African American History: A Very Short Introduction

VERY SHORT INTRODUCTIONS are for anyone wanting a stimulating and accessible way into a new subject. They are written by experts, and have been translated into more than 45 different languages.

The series began in 1995, and now covers a wide variety of topics in every discipline. The VSI library currently contains over 700 volumes—a Very Short Introduction to everything from Psychology and Philosophy of Science to American History and Relativity—and continues to grow in every subject area.

Very Short Introductions available now:

Available soon:

For more information visit our website

www.oup.com/vsi/

Jonathan Scott Holloway

AFRICAN AMERICAN HISTORY

A Very Short Introduction

OXFORD
UNIVERSITY PRESS

Oxford University Press is a department of the University of Oxford.
It furthers the University's objective of excellence in research, scholarship,
and education by publishing worldwide. Oxford is a registered trade mark of
Oxford University Press in the UK and certain other countries.

Published in the United States of America by Oxford University Press
198 Madison Avenue, New York, NY 10016, United States of America.

Library of Congress Cataloging-in-Publication Data

Names: Holloway, Jonathan Scott, author.
Title: African American history : a very short introduction / Jonathan Scott Holloway.
Other titles: Cause of freedom
Description: New York, NY : Oxford University Press, [2023] |
Series: Very short introductions | "Published in hardcover as "The Cause of Freedom:
A Concise History of African Americans" (2021)." |
Includes bibliographical references and index.
Identifiers: LCCN 2022041704 (print) | LCCN 2022041705 (ebook) |
ISBN 9780190915155 (paperback) | ISBN 9780190915179 (epub) |
ISBN 9780190915186
Subjects: LCSH: African Americans—History. | African Americans—Civil
rights—History. | United States—Race relations—History.
Classification: LCC E185 .H565 2023 (print) | LCC E185 (ebook) |
DDC 973/.0496073—dc23/eng/20220920
LC record available at https://lccn.loc.gov/2022041704
LC ebook record available at https://lccn.loc.gov/2022041705

1 3 5 7 9 8 6 4 2

Printed and bound by
CPI Group (UK) Ltd, Croydon, CR0 4YY

*For the next generation, no matter where
on the road they may be:
Yvette, David, Caitlyn, Victoria, Brian, John, Wendell,
Hank, Luke, Zoe, Emerson, Ellison, and Max*

The cause of freedom is not the cause of a race or a sect, a party or a class—it is the cause of human kind, the very birthright of humanity.

—Anna Julia Cooper, *A Voice From The South* (1892)

Contents

List of illustrations

Acknowledgments

Although this is a short book, I received a lot of support in the process of its becoming. I must start these acknowledgments with Lucy Caplan. Lucy graciously signed on to this project while she was wrapping up her dissertation and stayed with it even after earning her degree. While Lucy is an incredibly talented writer and editor, she was also an important conceptual collaborator, and this project is considerably better for her suggestions and insights.

Lara Beise deserves special recognition. We have worked together for six years now. All the while, she has patiently managed my time so that I can take on additional projects while still meeting my administrative duties. Lara facilitated the completion of this project in substantive ways and I am beholden to her for her steadfast assistance.

I also want to thank all of the students I've had the honor to teach in my survey course, "African American History: Emancipation to the Present." What I learned from them, as well as from the graduate students who helped me run the course for almost two decades, has shaped this book in significant ways.

While the conceptual roots of this project are based in those lecture courses at Yale University, I am grateful for the research support at Northwestern and Rutgers that allowed me to develop and then bring this project to completion.

Finally, I acknowledge my family: Aisling, Emerson, and Ellison. Working on this book during my "free time" meant that I was less available for them. I choose to believe that they viewed this as a loss for which they had to find their own compensation. But that, I realize, may just be my version of history. Whatever the truth happens to be, I remain grateful to these amazing people all the same.

Introduction: What does it mean to be American?

In telling the story of the African American past, *The Cause of Freedom* demonstrates how difficult it is to answer this question. Even if we ignore for a moment that the history of the African American presence in North America predates the establishment of this country by over 150 years, we are left with a puzzle: the United States of America takes great pride in its commitment to freedom and yet somehow accepted the preservation of slavery in its founding documents. Similarly, in a country that places so much rhetorical importance on the equality of opportunity, we have reconciled ourselves too easily to the sense that there's little more to be done to make accommodations for the structural inequalities that were birthed by racialized slavery and that remain with us in the present day.

Deciding what it means to be American, however, does not go far enough in terms of capturing the totality of the African American past. Other deceptively brief questions invite similarly complicated answers. For example, because the African American past predates the founding of the United States, and because that pre-Declaration history is overwhelmingly defined by the daily brutalities associated with racialized slavery, it is useful to pose the broader question *What does it mean to be human?* Asking this question helps us gain insight into the English settlers' mindset as they justified creating a system of racialized chattel slavery in colonial Virginia to replace the system of indentured servitude that they brought with them when they initially crossed the Atlantic.

Connecting the question about humanity and Americanness—and in so doing linking the English settlers in Jamestown, Virginia, to the newly self-declared Americans in Philadelphia, Pennsylvania, some 150 years later—is another conjecture: *What does it mean to be a citizen?* This question, still being asked today, guides us toward an understanding of how the presence of enslaved Africans created an existential crisis for those who disagreed about the boundaries of freedom. Even for abolitionists who believed that slavery was a sin, the breadth of what was meant by freedom for enslaved Africans was a deeply contested idea. That contest was a conceptual one as much as it was literal. The increasing ideological tension between northern and southern states regarding the role of a slave system in the nation's economic and political spheres turned into the national bloodletting of the early 1860s. Roughly 750,000 Americans would die in the Civil War, a dispute, at its core, about who could be considered human, a citizen, and an American.

The issue of American citizenship, of belonging, is at the beating heart of the civil rights disputes that have erupted regularly in the more than 150 years since the end of the Civil War. While these disputes were made manifest over questions like equal access to transportation, high-quality education, healthcare, housing, and the ballot box, soon after the Civil War ended a different question began to be asked that echoed the debates about enslaved Africans' humanity: *What does it mean to be civilized?* This question, born in the early years of this country's industrial age and its dawning global ambitions, invited the most mean-spirited answers that were deployed to justify denying African Americans the fruits of American citizenship. In more instances than historians have been able to count, answers to this question came in the form of domestic terrorism that was designed to ensure that African Americans remained perpetually insecure and unable to assert their claims to their national birthright without risking their jobs, their homes, and even their lives.

While all of the questions listed here beg long and nuanced answers that travel beyond the boundaries of this short history, there is one thing that is unambiguously clear: when one ventures into even a concise history of the African American past, one discovers that African Americans have always wanted to be considered human, citizens, American, and civilized. Further, they have wanted all the rights, responsibilities, and privileges associated with these recognitions.

One of the great challenges in meeting these desires has been the abiding failure to acknowledge African Americans' active role in making this nation and in articulating their own past. This failure to recognize African Americans' contributions has come at a great existential cost. The writer James Baldwin understood as much when, in 1965, he soberly declared, "It comes as a great shock to discover the country which is your birthplace and to which you owe your life and your identity has not in its whole system of reality evolved any place for you."

It is worth noting that the very idea of a history of the African American past is complicated ideological terrain that resonates with the questions that guide this book. At the center of this undulating landscape is the question "Who merits a history?" It may seem strange to ask this now, but it was not long ago that scholars believed a true record of the black past was unobtainable, insisting that there weren't any written records relating to the enslaved past and that any cultural ties that could connect enslaved Africans to the African continent did not survive the brutalities of slavery. These claims have been proven wrong.

One of the earliest proponents of a discernible African American past was Carter G. Woodson, founder of the Association for the Study of Negro Life and History in 1915 and publisher of the

Journal of Negro History. In 1926, Woodson established "Negro History Week," an effort to call attention to figures of the black past who played critical roles in the shaping of the nation. (Negro History Week would be rechristened "Black History Week" and then, in 1976, recognized by the federal government as "Black History Month.") Woodson fought many lonely battles, but he was undaunted in his life's work. Before he died in 1950, he began to see a slow but steady rise in the number of scholars studying the African American past. That growth has continued, and researching and teaching black history are familiar (but not ubiquitous) in primary, secondary, and higher education.

The title of this short history is drawn from a remark by Anna Julia Cooper, the educator and feminist who wrote the landmark 1892 book *A Voice from the South.* She observed, "The cause of freedom is not the cause of a race or a sect, a party or a class—it is the cause of human kind, the very birthright of humanity." Because African Americans were so often denied access to the benefits of the nation's founding principles, they had a special ability, something scholar-activist W. E. B. Du Bois called a "second-sight," to understand the contradictions baked into the nation's rhetoric. They could see that their fight for freedom may have had special implications for their day-to-day existence, but that it was a fight for every American because once African Americans secured that true freedom, it would mean that people of all backgrounds, immigrants, the poor, and the uneducated would have won theirs as well.

The history that follows opens on the shores of Jamestown in 1619 when the first group of Africans arrived in that settlement. It carries forward to the Black Lives Matter movement, a grassroots activist convulsion that declared in many ways that African Americans' present and past have value and meaning. I am writing this introduction during the four hundredth anniversary of that particular Jamestown arrival and at a moment when political debates have been rekindled about the nation's obligation to acknowledge and perhaps even repair its original sin of racialized slavery.

In 1965 Baldwin asked, "If one has got to prove one's title to the land, isn't 400 years enough?" This question, along with the others that are central to this history, seems so simple, but is laden with a complexity that tells a story about our own capacity and willingness to ever realize the ideal articulated in the country's founding document, namely that all people were created equal.

Chapter 1

Race, slavery, and ideology in colonial North America

In August 1619 a Dutch privateer, a sailing vessel whose crew had been conducting maritime raids in the West Indies for months, dropped anchor in the James River, seeking provisions. In exchange for food and supplies, the captain of the ship gave the governor of Jamestown Colony twenty Africans (whom the captain had likely seized from a Portuguese slave ship in the Caribbean). In popular culture, these twenty people are memorialized as the first African slaves in North America. However, while the arrival and sale of these individuals serve as a critical marker in the longer history of African Americans in the United States, they were not the first Africans on the continent, nor were they slaves.

European powers—Spain, Portugal, France, the Netherlands—had been exploring North and South America as well as the Caribbean for close to a century before the English established their first permanent base in Jamestown Colony, in 1607. The most famous African in this regard is Estevanico (also referred to as Esteban), who was one of four survivors of a Spanish-funded expedition that landed in 1528 on what is now the west coast of Florida. After its arrival, the expedition team was decimated by the environment and indigenous people who fought to protect their land. Estevanico was captured and enslaved, but eventually escaped and joined with fellow survivor Álvar Núñez Cabeza de Vaca on a mission to reach Mexico City. The record of their eight-year journey is one of the very first accounts of an African traveling across North America.

Eighty years after Estevanico's death, the twenty Africans were brought ashore in Jamestown. Unlike the records we have from Estevanico and Cabeza de Vaca, which are rich and detailed, what we know about the life experiences of those first Africans in Jamestown is frustratingly sparse. We do know that they were purchased, that they worked alongside English laborers who were brought to the colony as indentured servants, and that they survived harsh working conditions that extended much longer than the typical seven-year contract associated with indentured servitude. We also know that their importation was the beginning of an increasing traffic in unfree African labor in the English colonies and that the pace, scope, and scale of that traffic would increase dramatically as the demand for labor similarly increased throughout the colonized Atlantic world.

Much of the labor in the English colonies existed as indentured service. In order to pay off the cost of their transatlantic passage and earn their freedom, white European workers were required to labor for seven years in the colonies. For these workers, life opportunities were so limited at home that the chance for a new beginning and, in time, independence was too enticing to ignore. As they would soon discover, conditions in the colonies were unforgiving and, given the resistance that indigenous populations exerted against the European settlers, dangerous. All that said, for the African workforce, life in the English colonies was substantially more challenging than that experienced by the average European indentured servant. While there are records, even in Jamestown, of unfree African laborers earning their independence and acquiring property, there were decades of ambiguity about what it meant to be African in colonial North America. You could be an indentured servant, a slave, a free person, or even in rare instances a slave owner. However, as the demand for labor increased and as the population of the colonies grew, the ambiguity about the state of African labor began to diminish, and not in the Africans' favor.

By midcentury, colonial societies in the Americas had adopted unfree labor systems that relied upon religious, cultural, and physical differences. The logic behind each step in the shaping and implementation of these systems was as convenient as it was increasingly brutal. To start, practices that allowed unfree Africans to secure their freedom began to weaken as it became more difficult to recruit European workers to the colonies. From the property owner's perspective, being able to own access to someone's labor for that person's life allowed the owner to manage his resources with greater efficiency. The evolving mindset aligned neatly with and laid the foundation for the interdependence of unfree labor and capitalism.

Further facilitating the move toward lifetime servitude was the moral relaxation around the propriety of Christian slavery. New England Puritans were already at peace with the practice of slavery because the Bible made clear that slavery was permissible. In 1641 Massachusetts Bay Colony was the first English colony to recognize the legality of slavery. This law did not assign a racial aspect to slavery, but in the following years other English colonies went further than the Puritans in terms of instituting a slave system logic that explicitly targeted Africans. The clear turning point came in the 1660s with the propagation of slave codes addressing a range of matters. In 1662, for example, Virginia declared that the freedom of children born in the colony would be determined by the status of the mother. The significance of this change was immediate: from that point forward, slavery became an inherited status in Virginia. It also meant that the sexual exploitation of enslaved women by free white men was codified and legitimized. Other colonial statutes emerged that, taken together, built an economic system that increasingly relied upon enslaved people who held diminishing rights, whose children were born directly into servitude, and for whom being Christian afforded no physical protection. And quite distinct from the "race-blind" slave system originally rationalized by the Puritans, these new slave codes made it clear that black people were the intended targets. In less than two generations, then, slavery became racialized and hereditary in the English colonies.

Long before North American colonial legislatures took these steps, there were thriving societies in sub-Saharan Africa in which slavery was present. As historian Heather Williams points out, slavery functioned in a different register in these societies. People found themselves enslaved because they had been captured in wars or raids or as punishment for crimes. One's status as an enslaved person was not necessarily passed down through birth, however, and most enslaved people held domestic jobs in their captors' villages and farms, while some were exchanged for goods and materials that ran along the sub-Saharan trade routes.

The tenor of that trade changed in the early 1400s when Portuguese explorers began to appear along the western African coast, navigating inlets, going upriver, and working with local leaders to secure commodities and unfree labor to bring home. Over the course of the next two centuries, Dutch, Swedes, French, British, and Danes arrived and established their respective military, economic, and administrative presence, which stretched from modern-day Senegal to Angola. This presence was definitively embodied in the European fortifications that dotted the western African coast. Impressive coastal buildings that dominated the landscape, these structures resembled castles with their impregnable walls, large courtyards, military barracks, and mounted cannons. Their storerooms were originally designed to house precious metals, ivory, mahogany, pepper, gold, cloth, brass, and salt. However, when Europeans became aware of the demand for unfree labor in the New World, those basement storerooms were converted into dungeons.

This highly condensed narrative should not be taken as a suggestion that the turn toward slave trading as a major European strategy was free from complication or resistance. In fact, slave traders met resistance at every moment of the process. Enslaved Africans would rebel against their captors while they were en route to the coastal fortresses where slave ships were waiting to collect their human cargo. Those who were unable to escape found themselves in one of the dozens of fortresses along the coastline, forced into rank and fetid dungeons. Captives fought their imprisonment regularly, but were met with brutal and public displays of force that were meant to instill fear among other captives. If they survived the dungeons, they were forced through the so-called doors of no return and transferred to the holds of slave ships anchored offshore. The resistance did not end there, though, as captains' logs regularly made note of captives' efforts to start mutinies, of hunger strikes, and in the most horrible of circumstances, of suicides when captives threw themselves overboard.

Captains' and ship physicians' records catalog a list of miseries that Africans were forced to endure while they were crossing the Atlantic. They were crammed into the ships' holds, forced to lie down in rows, unable even to shift from one side to the other, stacked in horizontal columns where they were victim to the vomit, blood, and other bodily excretions of strangers above them, and chained together at all times, sometimes waking to discover the person to whom they were shackled had died overnight. Historians often cite Alexander Falconbridge, a ship's surgeon, who regularly visited the holds where the enslaved Africans were kept and documented his experience: "The deck was so covered with the blood and mucus which had proceeded from them in consequence of the flux, that it resembled a slaughterhouse." He continued, "It is not in the power of the human imagination to picture a situation more dreadful or disgusting."

There are very few records of what is referred to as the "Middle Passage" that were written by Africans themselves. The most

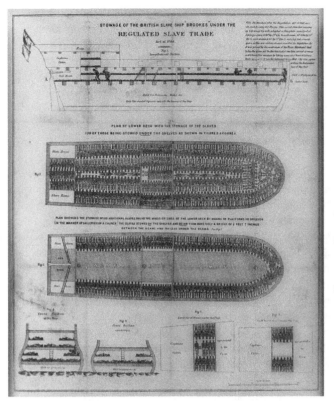

1. Created in 1787 and widely circulated in Britain by the Society for
Effecting the Abolition of the Slave Trade, this image of the hold of a
slave ship implores the viewer to confront the cramped conditions
and brutal cruelty that enslaved people endured during the Middle
Passage.

famous memoir of that experience was written by Olaudah
Equiano, born in what is now Nigeria, kidnapped when he was
a child, and sold repeatedly until he purchased his freedom at
the age of twenty-one. Equiano's prose is restrained, but his
experiences on the slave vessel that took him across the Atlantic
were nonetheless indelible: "the stench of the hold while we were

on the coast was so intolerably loathsome, that it was dangerous to remain there for any time, and some of us had been permitted to stay on the deck for the fresh air; but now that the whole ship's cargo were confined together, it became absolutely pestilential." (While Equiano's narrative is valuable to historians, we suffer from the fact that there are no extant narratives written by women who survived the transatlantic crossing. This absence means that the archive of this experience is incomplete in important ways.)

Historians will never know the exact number of Africans who were captured, sold into slavery, and then packed into slave ships bound for the Americas. Captains' logs have proved useful for developing a strong approximation of the scale of the transatlantic trafficking. In 1999 historian David Eltis released the Trans-Atlantic Slave Trade Database, drawing from records related to 36,000 individual slaving expeditions beginning in 1514 and running through the official end of the Atlantic slave trade in 1866. On the basis of this data, Eltis concludes that approximately 12.5 million enslaved people departed from the African coast in this time period. Ten million disembarked in the Americas. The history of the 2.5 million who did not survive the Middle Passage is metaphorically found on the floor of the Atlantic Ocean.

Most captive Africans found themselves in locations ranging anywhere from modern-day Buenos Aires to several major ports on the east coast of South America, continuing north through Jamaica and Cuba. No matter where they disembarked in South America and the Caribbean, enslaved Africans encountered the most physically punishing and cruel labor environment in the New World. In those areas, enslaved indigenous workers—mostly laboring in the sugarcane fields—were dying at alarming rates from overwork and disease. Importing wave after wave of enslaved Africans was the only solution that the colonists could muster. "Creative" means of torture became part of daily life as overseers sought new ways to motivate their captive laborers. John Hope

Franklin and Evelyn Brooks Higginbotham refer to the Brazilian *tronco*, *libambo*, *novena*, and *trezena* as examples. The first involved holding the enslaved person's ankles in place for several days, the second method was the same but the arms were held, and the last two were devices that held the worker face down to be beaten for nine and thirteen consecutive nights respectively. (Over half of the Africans who arrived in the New World ended up in Brazil.)

Although it does not diminish the horror of enslavement, the actual number of enslaved Africans who disembarked in mainland North America was relatively small in comparison with the full scale of the Atlantic slave trade. Of the 12.5 million who were taken from Africa, Eltis projects that close to 390,000 came to what is now the United States. Another 90,000 did not survive the Middle Passage.

Surviving the Middle Passage was but a phase in a series of grotesque challenges. Arriving in North America did not mean stepping onto shore and being handed to a master to begin work. First, individuals had to be inspected to make sure that they were healthy. Considering that the slave ships were frequently overrun with smallpox, cholera, and other communicable diseases, their human cargo were often quarantined for weeks before they were released to the mainland.

The most prominent site for quarantine in North America was Sullivan's Island, just off the coast from Charleston, South Carolina. Here diseased Africans would find themselves moved into "pesthouses," where they remained in quarantine until they could be incorporated into the larger captive community being prepared for auction. These houses were small, uncomfortable, multiroomed holding areas where they remained until the disease had run its course. This experience was not known to only a few Africans. The general consensus is that 40 percent of the enslaved Africans who entered North America came through Sullivan's Island, making Charleston the largest slave port in North

America. As one scholar put it, Sullivan's Island was a "macabre Ellis Island" for African Americans.

The quarantine served another purpose as well. It allowed slave merchants to prepare their captives for market. The traders wanted to make sure that the captives regained some of the weight they had lost during the Middle Passage, grooming them and oiling their bodies so that they would appear robust and healthy when it came time to go to auction. The enslaved Africans were, in so many ways, treated like animals being fattened for slaughter.

It had to have been bewildering and terrifying to leave Sullivan's Island and find yourself brought to market. Everything around you would have reinforced the uncertainty of the moment. Foreign languages, customs, dress, flora, fauna, and diet would be only the start of the confusion. Being poked and prodded by merchants, being stripped naked, and then suffering further degradation in order to satisfy the curious—these were standard practices in the slave marketplace.

Whether one went through Charleston or not, being sold into labor was an ending and a beginning. It marked the completion of the Middle Passage, certainly, but there was a robust intracontinental trade and enslaved individuals found themselves being moved from place to place, typically without warning. Sales were ordered to cover debts, to remove "difficult" laborers (those deemed "lazy" or those who were disruptive and posed a threat to the status quo) from a local worksite, to curry political and social favor, and to raise cash for future investments. The disorientation that was built into capture, diaspora, and arrival never ceased.

Even if one could ignore the psychological confusion of the moment, there is no moving beyond the fact that young women's bodies were commodified when they were being assessed for sexual and reproductive value. Then there was the sheer horror visited upon parents, primarily women, of being separated from their children at the point of sale.

While these aspects of the slave system—dehumanization, disorientation, commodification—universally applied wherever slavery took root, the types of labor that enslaved Africans performed varied widely. Although slavery was first legalized in New England, the number of enslaved Africans was lower in that region than in other areas in North America. Most enslaved workers did domestic work in households or learned trades that were of value in the small cities along the New England coast, as blacksmiths, painters, shoemakers, and such.

In the Mid-Atlantic region and then farther into the South, forced labor took on a decidedly different orientation. In those areas, enslaved Africans were used in agriculture and the structural economy that surrounded it. They cleared forests; built roads and eventually rail lines; raised plantation houses, slave quarters, stables, and barns; supported white planters and their families; fed everyone on the property; and more than anything else, worked the land. Not all southern agriculture was based on plantations; there were far more modest homesteads with fewer than five enslaved laborers tending to various needs, much as they would have done in New England. However, with each passing decade, the political and socioeconomic power in the South became more highly concentrated in the hands of plantation owners. The majority of enslaved Africans were to be found on plantations, and their labor was increasingly valuable given the southern economy's reliance upon the global demand for tobacco, rice, and eventually cotton.

Plantation farming was substantially different from that based in smaller landholdings. On large plantations, Africans worked in teams that were managed by white overseers. Cultivating tobacco, rice, and cotton was grueling work, and overseers became known for pushing the workers as hard as they possibly could in order to maximize the plantation's profits. Plantations with absentee landlords were particularly dangerous places for enslaved Africans to work. In those instances, the overseer was merely an employee himself and had little vested interest in protecting the owner's property. The use of the whip became a staple of plantation life. It was deployed in the belief that strict discipline would generate more productive labor. It was also used as a means of terrorizing a population into abject compliance. Rape, too, was used as a means of social control, just as it was an articulation of warped pleasure for the perpetrators.

There are many stories one can tell about slavery that raise important questions about the extent to which people were willing to rationalize abhorrent behavior. There are also ironies that tell us a lot about our national values. Historian Edmund Morgan argued this point in *American Slavery, American Freedom*. He charted the changes in seventeenth-century Virginia law regarding the nature of slavery while also observing the heightened rhetoric around the value of freedom. His main point was elegant and damning: the ideal of freedom, which would become the organizing principle of the United States, was reliant upon the growth of slavery. Much of freedom's meaning and value came from the fact that those who were free lived their lives in close proximity to the absolute denial of freedom. Further, as slavery became racialized, whites understood that the color of their skin had material consequences that were dependent upon slavery's perpetuation.

This was not just a feeling held by Virginians; it became an ideology throughout British North America. This ideology was propagated so successfully because enslaved Africans could be easily disregarded in any space that was unrelated to their physical labor. One example from colonial New England illustrates the breadth and depth of the colonists' commitment to the belief that enslaved Africans could not ever be their peers.

Phillis Wheatley, a native of western Africa, was captured as a child. She survived the Middle Passage and arrived in Boston in 1761, when John Wheatley purchased her. Phillis served as a domestic servant to Susanna Wheatley, who in turn taught her to read and write English. Susanna introduced Phillis to poetry, and the young domestic servant developed a talent for the form. Wheatley's poems began to appear in the region's newspapers and she soon became a local celebrity. By the early 1770s Wheatley was internationally known, partly for her poetry and partly because people viewed her as a curiosity: an enslaved person with intellect enough to compose creative literature? In 1773 Wheatley accompanied her master's son to England, where she hoped to find a press willing to publish her poetry. Although she enjoyed support from leading British figures, Wheatley had to undergo an examination and then secure an attestation from leading Bostonians that she was, in fact, the author of the poems in question. With that final piece of support in place, Wheatley published *Poems on Subjects, Religious and Moral* in late 1773, becoming the first African woman to publish a book of poetry in the Americas. Not all colonial leaders, however, were similarly enlightened. When asked a few years later about Wheatley's poetry, Thomas Jefferson, at that point the author of the Declaration of Independence, declared, "The compositions published under her name are below the dignity of criticism."

There are many other examples that illuminate the fundamental ironies embedded in the narrative of American exceptionalism. The denial of Phillis Wheatley's human and civic potential on the grounds of her race and the condition of servitude that had been forced upon her, however, is particularly galling given the colonists' simultaneous determination to secure their own freedom. That these refusals took place in the same physical spaces where the American Revolutionary War would begin a few years later is further evidence of the new nation's commitment to ignoring its own deep inconsistencies.

In the years between the Declaration of Independence and the ratification of the Constitution, the United States moved from being a concept to a country. The debates about the power of state governments, the role and authority of a federal government, and the creation of a national judiciary offer a fascinating portrait of a people determining the possibilities of their freedom as well as the limits on that freedom that they were willing to endure. What one does not find in that portrait, however, is a sensitivity to the possibilities of freedom for those who were systematically denied it. In fact, with little more than a moment's glance, an image that is quite the opposite appears.

The Constitution was a remarkable document for the ways in which it delineated a country that would eschew the trappings of monarchy and would be led by representatives of the country's citizens. The authors of the Constitution spoke to the issue of citizens' voice in the new representative government. In an effort to appease the delegates from the slaveholding states who were threatening to derail the Constitutional Convention, a compromise was reached regarding the apportionment of representatives and taxes. The result: written into the first article of the Constitution was the declaration that each enslaved person would count as three-fifths of a person, thereby increasing the size of the southern population and, thus, southern representative power. This three-fifths compromise did nothing to benefit enslaved people, of course, as they were not to be considered citizens.

Later, in Article 4, the delegates to the convention rationalized the idea that slavery had a proper place in the new country. The Constitution declared that self-emancipating people ("runaway slaves" in the popular parlance) had no rights to freedom, even in those parts of the country where slavery had been declared illegal. The rhetorical irony that this would be a nation bound by freedom was lost on the authors of these founding documents.

The accumulating effects of the authority given to the new nation's states, the overprivileging of southern representation, and the protection that allowed slave owners to cross state lines in pursuit of self-emancipated people were mortally significant. The consequences were decades in coming, but what many considered the outgrowth of a rational politics of compromise turned out to be the preparation of the soil, the planting of the seed, and the nurturing of a crop that would burst forth as the sectional crisis leading to the Civil War.

The most important author of this nation's founding document was Thomas Jefferson. A passionate defender of liberty and of states' rights, Jefferson embodied the bitter ironies and illogics that were built into the country's foundation. He criticized King George for promoting slavery in the English colonies, but he himself owned as many as six hundred slaves; he believed that enslaved people should be emancipated, but he freed only two of his laborers while he was alive and, as stipulated in his will, freed another five upon his death; finally, Jefferson was deeply opposed to the mixing of the races, but there is overwhelming evidence that Jefferson partnered with his slave Sally Hemings and fathered her six children.

Scholars have been fighting over Jefferson's contradictions for over three hundred years now. Reading his 1785 book, *Notes on the State of Virginia*, doesn't clear up matters. In one moment, the reader finds Jefferson delineating differences between the races that resonate loudly and sympathetically with the brute force arguments of white supremacy. Yet elsewhere, Jefferson perceptively discusses the absurdities of the slave economy, anticipating today's ideological and racial battles: "Deep rooted prejudices entertained by the whites; ten thousand recollections, by the blacks, of the injuries they have sustained; new provocations; the real distinctions which nature has made...will divide us into parties, and produce convulsions which will probably never end."

The injuries, of course, were real. They came in the form of a denial of one's claims to citizenship status, in the form of disbelief regarding human capability, in the form of the whip ripping into bare flesh, in the form of the invasive clinical examinations when one was standing on the auction block, and in the form of the ships' holds where one was shackled before crossing the Atlantic Ocean. Olaudah Equiano's words are a powerful reminder of the deep wounds inflicted by this brutalizing and dehumanizing system. Recalling the scene when he first went below deck on the slave ship that carried him to the new world, Equiano wrote, "The shrieks of the women, and groans of the dying, rendered the whole a scene of horror most inconceivable."

The Interesting Narrative of the Life of Olaudah Equiano was an instant sensation when it was published in Britain. Although Equiano would not live to see his abolitionist ambitions realized, his memoir would play an important role in the rise of the international antislavery movement. *The Interesting Narrative* was published in 1789, eight years before Equiano died. It bears noting that the US Constitution, the instantiation of the ideas articulated in the Declaration of Independence, Thomas Jefferson's masterwork, was ratified that same year.

Chapter 2

Resistance and African American identity before the Civil War

In the spring of 1852 Frederick Douglass, easily the most prominent African American abolitionist and leader in the nineteenth century, received an invitation from the Rochester (New York) Ladies' Anti-Slavery Society to address their group on Independence Day. The members hoped that he would talk to them about freedom, liberty, and national greatness. Douglass, who told the story of his self-emancipation in his popular 1845 autobiography *Narrative of the Life of Frederick Douglass*, accepted the invitation but refused to join them on July Fourth. The reasons for his refusal became quite evident in his three-hour-long speech. Douglass pointed out the hypocrisy of inviting a self-emancipated person to speak with admiration about US independence. "This Fourth of July is yours, not mine," Douglass thundered. "You may rejoice, I must mourn. To drag a man in fetters into the grand illuminated temple of liberty, and call upon him to join you in joyous anthems, were inhuman mockery and sacrilegious irony. Do you mean, citizens, to mock me, by asking me to speak today?"

Douglass addressed the irony of the institution of slavery in a nation that was predicated on freedom and equality of opportunity. In this way, Douglass was part of a tradition of African American writing, thinking, and activism that exposed the hypocrisy of the American experiment. This tradition was a contributing element to political, social, and religious movements that began to cohere in the nineteenth century as slavery expanded. These movements, many local and limited, others operating on a wider and more ambitious scale, captured much of the African American experience in the antebellum period—the years between the ratification of the Constitution and the start of the Civil War. African Americans, whether enslaved or free, were active participants in the shaping of their own future as well as the nation's. Although they were treated horribly, African Americans relentlessly pushed to have their individual humanity recognized and, at the level of the body politic, their citizenship respected.

Frederick Douglass's own history of resistance and education is illuminating. Douglass was born into slavery in 1818. His mother was enslaved, and his father was white and likely his master. Douglass was separated from his mother at an early age, and by the time he was eight, he had been sold, moving from a plantation in eastern Maryland to Baltimore. There, his owner's wife began to teach him to read, until her husband convinced her that literacy would encourage a desire for freedom. Douglass persisted, however, and taught himself to read. Then, in an act of radical independence, Douglass began to teach other enslaved people how to read. Once he was discovered, he was sent to a plantation where Edward Covey, an infamous slave driver, attempted to break Douglass by subjecting him to a year of orchestrated beatings.

Two years after his return, Douglass developed a plan to secure his freedom, and with the help of a network of free blacks, secretly traveled from Baltimore to Philadelphia and on to New York City. Very soon, the talented Douglass honed his writing and speaking skills and began a decades-long career as a writer, newspaper editor, antislavery activist, and women's rights activist. (His commitment to women's rights—most prominently declared when he attended the Seneca Falls Convention in 1848—is partly why the Ladies' Anti-Slavery Society of Rochester invited him to speak before their group in July 1852.) After the Civil War, Douglass remained in public life and was the most prominent African American leader in the country until his death in 1895. It bears noting that in the decades between the time he gained his freedom and the end of the Civil War, Douglass was, in the eyes of the law, a fugitive slave.

Douglass, of course, was not the only fugitive slave in the country. Every year, hundreds of enslaved people would escape their bondage, their eyes on freedom. Escape was the riskiest and most extreme form of resistance to the slave regime. A self-emancipated person was an affront to a system that aspired to achieve total control. In order to maintain that control, southern planters went to great expense to organize and deploy slave patrols to track down runaways. For the owners, runaway slaves embodied lost labor as well as lost property. Further, self-emancipated people were a threat since they became symbols of possibility for those who remained enslaved.

The idea of total control was critical to the perpetuation of the slave political economy. And while that concept held sway in popular thought, the fact is that enslaved people were constantly pushing against the system that stole their labor and attempted to deprive them of their humanity. There were daily acts of resistance in which the enslaved person remained in place—slowing the work pace, breaking tools, stealing property—and then there were the considerably bolder attempts to escape. In the latter case, most escapes would last only a few days, as the roaming slave patrols, the physically punishing natural surroundings, and the lack of food or shelter usually meant that a return to the worksite was the only viable option. We will never know the names of all those who found ways to resist the conditions that set the terms of their daily life, but we know enough from the archival material to conclude that the notion of the happy, docile slave is one of the most absurd myths about the nation's past.

In addition to such individual acts of resistance, there was a long record of organized resistance at local and international levels. On a Sunday morning in 1739 in South Carolina, a group of about twenty enslaved people assembled near the Stono River. Led by a man named Jemmy, the group killed two white shopkeepers, seized the store's weapons and ammunition, and proceeded to march toward Spanish Florida, where they hoped to secure their freedom. Gathering more supporters as they marched, the group eventually was intercepted by a white militia; in the ensuing battle, more than twenty white men and forty enslaved people were killed. Operating at a much larger scale, the Haitian Revolution began in 1791 and culminated in 1805. This rebellion liberated enslaved people in Haiti and ended French colonial rule, leading to the formation of the first independent black republic in the New World. Southern slaveholders were fearful that the success of the revolt would inspire similar events in the United States. So were federal lawmakers, who instituted a short-lived arms embargo on Haiti following the revolution. Although some voices did point out the obvious parallels between Haiti's quest for independence and the United States' own, Congress did not officially recognize the new nation's independence until 1862.

The dissonance between ideals and reality was not unique at the time. Given the Founding Fathers' rhetoric of liberty and narratives of freedom, it is ironic that in 1793 George Washington signed the first Fugitive Slave Act into law. This act allowed slaveholders to cross state lines in pursuit of self-emancipated people. Their only burden of proof was their personal testimony. In response to the 1793 Fugitive Slave Act, many northern states passed laws that protected their free African American citizens, requiring southern slaveholders to produce definitive evidence that the person they claimed as their property was, in fact, known to them.

The Fugitive Slave Act of 1793 and free states' responses to this federal mandate were an early articulation of the political and economic battles that would be waged throughout the antebellum period. Those battles intensified with the abolition of the transatlantic slave trade in 1808 and subsequent development of the domestic slave trade. Historians estimate that more than one million enslaved people were moved from the Upper South to the Deep South in the early years of the nineteenth century. Sometimes known as the "Second Middle Passage," this mass dislocation destroyed families and communities.

Those who were moved farther south faced much more daunting obstacles when it came to securing their freedom. The greater distance to free territory was the most obvious of these, but the increased intensity of white surveillance the farther one went south also made it more difficult to attempt escape. That did not diminish enslaved people's efforts to do so, however. Denmark Vesey is a case in point. Vesey lived in Charleston, South Carolina, and although he purchased his freedom in 1799 he remained in the area, socializing with the enslaved people in Charleston (there had always been a small free black population in the area). In 1820 Vesey and his friends developed plans to take the Charleston Armory, fight their way to a vessel, and sail to Haiti as free people. Vesey's plans were leaked to local white slave owners, who responded in force. Well over one hundred enslaved people and free blacks were arrested, with most sentenced to death. Two years after his plot was revealed, Vesey was publicly hanged with five coconspirators. More mass hangings followed that month.

The intensity of whites' reaction to Vesey's plan points to the undercurrent of anxiety that coursed throughout slave society. Because there were always rumors of escape plans and plots to attack the white overseers and masters and mistresses, there was an attendant "need" to demonstrate white domination and a resolve to control access to information. For example, just as Frederick Douglass had to be sent away from Baltimore because he was teaching other enslaved people to read, white

Charlestonians recognized that Denmark Vesey's literacy was a critical factor in his ability to plan for insurrection. As a response, state officials in South Carolina instituted a host of regulations that put further constraints on enslaved individuals' ability to move and congregate, strengthened existing law against teaching enslaved people to read, and increased surveillance of free blacks who lived in the state.

Other states joined South Carolina in a steady legislative march toward increasing restrictions on enslaved and free African Americans. Whites were afraid that African Americans would unite and make a determined claim on full emancipation and citizenship. There was good reason for southern whites to feel anxious in this regard. As the nation moved further into the nineteenth century, the rhetorical, political, and social calls for change only intensified. One key inflection point was encapsulated in the passage of the Missouri Compromise of 1820. The compromise took its name due to circumstance. Representatives from Missouri Territory had submitted a petition for statehood but wanted slavery to be permitted in the future state. Were Congress to accept Missouri under these conditions, however, slaveholding states would be in the majority, thus giving southern legislators more federal authority to expand slavery even more. The balance of political and economic power had to be maintained as the nation continued its westward march to the Pacific. A compromise was struck: Missouri could join the Union, but Maine, a free territory, would join as a state at effectively the same time. Further, slavery would be illegal in all US lands north of the 36°30′ parallel, excluding Missouri. Like the Compromise of 1850 that would follow thirty years later, the Missouri Compromise provided a political solution that kept the Union intact. For African Americans and their white antislavery allies, however, the political stability that grew out of the Missouri Compromise came at a steep price. Now, southerners had a new and federally sponsored authorization for a political and economic system predicated on slavery.

Amid these dispiriting circumstances, African Americans continued to call for change. David Walker's brief history is illustrative. Born free in Ohio in 1785, Walker had settled in Boston by 1825. There, he maintained a small clothing store while advocating for abolition with increasing determination. He sheltered fugitive enslaved people and wrote for *Freedom's Journal*, the first African American newspaper. He made a national name for himself in 1829 when he published a pamphlet titled *Walker's Appeal . . . to the Coloured Citizens of the World*.

Walker was alarmed by the rise and relative popularity of the American Colonization Society, a group founded in 1816 that sought to establish a colony in Africa to which enslaved African Americans could be sent, thus ridding the country of its original sin. For Walker, African Americans' place was in the United States, and they were not to be denied the opportunities that were afforded to all of the nation's citizens. Walker was in familiar abolitionist company with these observations. Where he differed, though, was in his militant tone:

> . . . we must exert ourselves to the full. For remember, that it is the greatest desire and object of the greater part of the whites, to keep us ignorant, and make us work to support them and their families. . . . Will any of us leave our homes and go to Africa? I hope not. Let them commence their attack. . . . Let no man of us budge one step, and let slave-holders come to beat us from our country. America is more our country, than it is the whites—we have enriched it with our *blood and tears*.

Walker's pamphlet electrified his readers and inspired many moderate white abolitionists to break from the American Colonization Society, recognizing that restitution had to be birthed and raised in the United States instead of being relegated to a continent that was largely unknown to African Americans. Walker died a year after publishing his *Appeal*, but the pamphlet remained influential. Its publication is seen as the start of the militant abolitionist phase of the antebellum era, when black and white abolitionists focused their call for immediate emancipation, with increasing numbers of them willing to secure freedom at any price.

Walker served as an inspiration for writer and activist Maria Stewart. She added a women's agenda to Walker's abolitionist arguments and was unafraid to criticize white allies for their failure to advocate forcefully for full equality of opportunity. In her 1832 speech "Why Sit Ye Here and Die?" Stewart spoke to the limits placed on African American women and the greater opportunity that white women enjoyed: "O, ye fairer sisters, whose hands are never soiled, whose nerves and muscles are never strained, go learn by experience! Had we had the opportunity that you have had, to improve our moral and mental faculties, what would have hindered our intellects from being as bright, and our manners from being as dignified as yours?"

Although there is no evidence that Nat Turner, an enslaved person in southern Virginia, ever read *Walker's Appeal*, he acted on his plan for self-emancipation two years after the pamphlet's publication. If Turner had emancipated just himself, it's unlikely we would know his name, but Turner, led by powerful messianic visions, organized a rebellion of roughly seventy enslaved people. Over the course of forty-eight hours, Turner and his followers murdered almost sixty white southerners. A Virginia militia captured the rebels but could not contain the retributive violence. Over the next two weeks, armed whites killed over one hundred African Americans, many of them having had nothing to do with the rebellion. This was a rough justice born of fear stoked by Walker's writing and Turner's visions. The violent white suppression did little to quell other uprisings, though, as Africans' and African Americans' desire for freedom and the right to control their own bodies inspired increasingly determined plans for self-emancipation.

Harriet Tubman's story emphasizes the persistence of the desire for freedom as well as the determination to secure it for others. Tubman first tried to secure her freedom when she was seven years old. Her mistress, who regularly beat her for the slightest transgression, caught her stealing a lump of sugar. Tubman fled, knowing that she was about to be whipped for her theft. She hid in a pigpen for days until hunger forced her back to her mistress. Two decades later, Tubman succeeded in emancipating herself, leaving Maryland for Philadelphia and the relative protections of the "Quaker City." In her escape, Tubman relied on an informal network of free blacks and sympathetic whites—colloquially known as the Underground Railroad. Over the course of the next decade, Tubman returned repeatedly to Maryland's Eastern Shore, securing freedom for close to one hundred enslaved people, taking them first to Philadelphia and later to Canada.

No one needed to explain the risks involved in self-emancipation to people like Harriet Jacobs. Raised in slavery in North Carolina, Jacobs was routinely sexually harassed by her owner throughout her teens. When she turned twenty-two, she decided to escape; but escape for her meant hiding in the crawl space of a house for seven years. In 1842 Jacobs managed to flee to Philadelphia, eventually settling in New York and then Boston, where she found work as a nanny. She would eventually write her autobiography, *Incidents in the Life of a Slave Girl*. When it was published in 1861, it was one of the first slave narratives to detail the sexual harassment that was part of daily life for black women.

Slave narratives like Jacobs's appealed to antislavery activists. The serial acts of inhumanity recounted in those texts did not align with abolitionists' views of a just and civil society. These narratives helped feed the propagation of abolitionist groups. African American–led antislavery societies abounded in the North. By the early 1820s, dozens of these groups could be found in northern cities. David Walker, the author of the *Appeal* that would electrify African American and white antislavery activists, was a founding

2. Most images of Harriet Tubman depict her as an older, frail woman, but this rare portrait captures her youthful strength: she stares unflinchingly at the camera, in a posture that exemplifies her lifelong bravery and courage.

member of one such group, the Massachusetts General Colored Association of Boston. Other groups emerged soon after.

In 1830 African American religious leaders, writers, politicians, businessmen, and educators met in Philadelphia with the goal of bettering African Americans' position and condition. The Colored Convention Movement grew out of this meeting, with future gatherings held mostly throughout the Northeast and Mid-Atlantic. Bishop Richard Allen, head of the African Methodist Episcopal Church, the first independent African American Protestant denomination (established in 1816), was elected president at the Philadelphia meeting and used his church and subsequent convention meetings as vehicles to advocate for black independence and to support and spread antislavery ideology.

While the Colored Convention Movement reflected an increasingly public and cohesive African American antislavery discourse, white allies were also major contributors to the highly charged political atmosphere. One of the most prominent individuals in this regard was William Lloyd Garrison, who published the first edition of his weekly newspaper, the *Liberator*, in January 1831. Garrison had already been a committed abolitionist, believing that a gradual end to slavery should be accompanied by African American emigration to Africa. After reading *Walker's Appeal*, however, Garrison announced his opposition to colonization and called for an immediate emancipation of all enslaved people. The *Liberator*, whose readership was overwhelmingly African American, ran for over thirty years, ceasing publication only when the official end of slavery was secured with the ratification of the Thirteenth Amendment to the Constitution. The newspaper would inspire other whites to get involved in the antislavery movement and would serve as a bully pulpit for white and African American abolitionists.

Frederick Douglass, already well known in abolitionist circles, took inspiration from Garrison's newspaper and started his own in 1847. Douglass used his newspaper, first known as the *North Star*, as a platform for offering commentary on contemporary events, with a special focus on the African American experience, the abolitionist project, and the moral failings of a southern political economic system that was anchored in forced labor. Through his work on the *North Star*, Douglass's public profile increased so much that in 1851 it made sense to change the name of the periodical to *Frederick Douglass's Paper*.

It would be a mistake, however, to believe that Douglass's ascent was linear and without controversy. While he was the most celebrated African American speaker and political activist of the age, this did not mean that all abolitionists were aligned in their views about the place that African Americans could occupy in the public sphere. A major strand of abolitionist thought revolved around colonization; another line of reasoning called for the immediate end of slavery and even the dismantling of the Constitution. Intersecting these camps within abolitionist circles were lines of racial sensibilities that often demonstrated to African Americans that many white abolitionist allies maintained very limited ideas about blacks' humanity, independence of mind and spirit, and abilities.

Even efforts to capture and retell the history of the abolitionist movement reflected the range of sensibilities found among the progressive allies. The recounting of prominent African American abolitionist, women's rights activist, and preacher Sojourner Truth is a case in point. In 1851 Truth gave an extemporaneous speech at the Ohio Women's Rights convention. That speech largely revolved around the importance of women's equality while also detailing the importance of the abolitionists' call for emancipation. The contemporary account of her speech noted that it was delivered calmly and was well received by an admiring crowd of mostly white supporters. Twelve years later Frances

Gage, one of the convention's organizers, offered a starkly different portrait of the speech and its reception. According to Gage, Truth excoriated audience members who didn't want her to speak and criticized those people who called for chivalric support for women but who limited that call to white women. Gage recalled that Truth spoke about the hardships she had endured as an enslaved person and then, generally, as an African American, while repeatedly daring the audience to answer the question "A'n't I a Woman?"

In Gage's account, Truth was able to deliver her speech against the hissing refrain of hostile audience members, asking them five times to recognize her as a woman. It was a powerful story that seemed to affirm Truth's dignity and humanity, but it came at the cost of likely being untrue. Gage's Truth spoke in broken southern dialect, while the actual Truth had been raised in upstate New York, speaking only Dutch until she was nine and always priding herself on her command of proper English. Further, none of the contemporary accounts of the speech make a single mention of the phrase "A'n't I a Woman?"

Truth's "A'n't I a Woman?" speech has become the dominant narrative that describes her contributions to African American resistance. Although an extemporaneous speech that was never transcribed opens itself up to a multiplicity of versions, the extreme differences in this case and the fact that the least accurate version is the one that resonated with the public make clear that even a sympathetic public needed African Americans to reside somewhere closer to illiteracy than not. Furthermore, this public needed African Americans to be benighted in some way, authentic in their poverty or limited education as if it were the natural state of the black mind.

Truth and Douglass fought endlessly against those stereotypes, as did other African American abolitionists, like Martin Delany. Delany cofounded the *North Star* with Douglass and traveled the

North fundraising for the paper and abolitionist causes. Frustrated by the pervasiveness and persistence of racist ideology and practices wherever he went, Delany came to believe that there was no hope for African Americans in the United States, and he embraced the idea of emigration (but not to Liberia, as that was the idea of white slaveholders and the ruling class; Delany had his eyes on Central and South America and the West Indies). Delany's new ideas about black possibilities in the United States and his calls for racial self-reliance dismayed Douglass and have led many historians to consider him the country's first black nationalist.

One can hear Delany's frustration and see his vision in his 1852 manifesto, *The Condition, Elevation, Emigration, and Destiny of the Colored People of the United States, Politically Considered*. Delany wrote, "The time has now fully arrived, when the colored race is called upon by all the ties of common humanity, and all the claims of consummate justice, to go forward and take their position, and do battle in the struggle now being made for the redemption of the world.... But we must go from among our oppressors; it never can be done by staying among them."

There is little coincidence in the fact that Truth's, Douglass's, and Delany's speeches and writings, all clustered in the first moments of the 1850s, were suffused with disdain, frustration, and despair. The contingent and fragile nature of black freedom had to have been personally and psychologically enervating. The midcentury tribulations of Dred Scott, an enslaved man who had lived with his master and mistress on both sides of latitude 36°30´ (the line established by the Missouri Compromise that separated free and slave states), underscored the cruelty that was woven into the political, social, and economic fabric of a nation that embraced the rhetoric of freedom while behaving in ways that suggested a different faith.

Upon his master's death in 1846, Scott sued for his freedom on the grounds that he had lived in free territory. Lower courts issued a series of conflicting decisions, and for eleven years Scott and his family lived in limbo: emancipated, re-enslaved, emancipated, re-enslaved.

Finally, in 1857, the Supreme Court ruled in *Scott v. Sandford*, better known as the "Dred Scott case," that Scott should remain enslaved. Chief Justice Roger B. Taney argued that Scott's status as an enslaved person meant that he was not a US citizen and therefore could not legally sue in a federal court. Moreover, Taney argued that as an enslaved person, Scott was personal property and could never become free. For Taney, African Americans were "so far inferior that they had no rights which a white man was bound to respect." Taney's decision infuriated antislavery advocates, angered the new Republican Party, and exacerbated national tensions. Meanwhile, Dred Scott lived out a bitter coda to a life of struggle. Scott's mistress eventually gave him and his family their freedom, but soon thereafter he contracted tuberculosis and died. His death came just one year after Taney had declared that Scott had no rights worth respecting.

At the same time that Dred Scott was caught in his tortuous legal struggle, Margaret Garner, an enslaved woman who fled with her family in 1856 across a frozen Ohio river to Cincinnati and freedom, found herself trapped in one of her own. Because Garner and her family were viewed as fugitives, they had to remain in hiding, waiting for safe passage to a place farther north, hopefully Canada. Before they could start that next leg of their journey, they were found by slave catchers. Moments before the slave catchers stormed the house where the family was hiding, Garner killed her two-year-old daughter instead of seeing her returned to slavery. She also tried to kill her other children and then herself but was unsuccessful.

The resulting legal case revolved around the question of the legality of the Fugitive Slave Law and the limits of federal authority against states' rights. Antislavery activists called for

Garner to be tried for murder as a free person in the state of Ohio (with a plan already in place for the governor to pardon her); their opponents declared that as an enslaved person she was nothing more than property and, in line with the Fugitive Slave Law, had to be returned to her owner. Federal law prevailed and Garner was returned to slavery in Kentucky. When lawyers from Ohio traveled to Kentucky to get her extradited back to Ohio to stand trial as a free person, they could not find her. Years later it would be discovered that Garner succumbed to tuberculosis just two years after her daughter's death. (Garner's story served as the inspiration for Toni Morrison's 1987 Pulitzer Prize–winning novel, *Beloved*.)

While testimony about the brutality of slavery has survived to the present day, it is impossible to know in deeply personal ways the psychological trauma that the system inflicted upon those in bondage. Stories like Garner's, however, bring us closer to an understanding of this trauma, as well as the lengths to which one could go in order to resist slavery and its horrors. While Garner's actions represent one extreme end of the spectrum of resistance, it is important to remember that African Americans, enslaved and free, constantly fought against the political and economic system of forced labor. This resistance could be intimate and physically violent or public and limited to rhetorical declarations. In either instance—and in every case in between—African Americans strove to be authors of their own destiny, always aspiring to be free and recognized as citizens despite the views of their enemies, too frequently shared by their allies and increasingly espoused in law.

Chapter 3
War, freedom, and a nation reconsidered

The question of what it meant to be an American took on new importance in the years leading up to, during, and after the Civil War. Similarly, the question of what it meant to be a citizen had to be reconsidered in the context of the destruction of a political and economic system that was predicated on denying people citizenship rights. A black presence played a significant role throughout these debates. This presence was expressed through whites' thoughts and actions with regard to blacks (what to do with this newly freed people?), or it was articulated in the active roles that African Americans played in claiming their place in society.

The Civil War began in April 1861 and continued through April 1865. While it lasted only four years, the toll on the country was horrific. More than 750,000 people died in the conflict, and much of the southern economic infrastructure was destroyed. The ideological battle, however, had started years before.

Local violence emerged when the Kansas–Nebraska Act of 1854 inspired pro- and antislavery forces to take up arms in their desire to shape the destiny of their respective regions. The white Connecticut-born abolitionist John Brown had moved to Kansas just after the Kansas–Nebraska Act had been passed and soon found himself wrapped up in the area's violence. Shocked that proslavery forces had taken over nearby Lawrence and sacked the town, he organized a small militia to conduct a retaliatory nighttime raid against other proslavery settlers, murdering them all. Historian James McPherson writes that witnesses said Brown had gone "crazy" at that moment. In the wake of his actions in Kansas, Brown became a "free-state guerilla chieftain."

Even though an unsteady peace in Kansas would begin in 1856, Brown was not stilled. He quietly developed a plan that he felt would lead to slave insurrections, the eventual end of slavery, and the creation of a black republic. In March 1859 Brown pulled together a band of armed abolitionists, white as well as black, with the goal of storming the arsenal in Harpers Ferry, Virginia. Brown sought support from his confidant Frederick Douglass, but Douglass rejected the plan as unfeasible. Brown was undeterred and launched the raid. Although his group secured the arsenal, the waves of self-emancipating people Brown believed would arrive to take up arms to escalate the battle never materialized.

A day after winning Harpers Ferry, Brown and his group were quickly defeated by troops serving under Colonel Robert E. Lee. Brown was wounded in the battle and captured. During the ensuing trial, Brown vaulted into the national consciousness and quickly became viewed as a messianic hero for antislavery ideologues. Brown fanned the flames of his celebrity with long soliloquies about the moral turpitude of slavery, but to no avail. Brown was convicted of treason and sentenced to be hanged. Upon his sentencing he declared, "I believe that to have interfered as I have done, as I have always freely admitted I have done, in behalf of His despised poor, is no wrong, but right."

John Brown's raid was a complete failure in a tactical sense, but Brown's martyrdom marked a major turning point in the ideological landscape. Heightened southern fears of insurrection compounded by a rising regional militarism led, as McPherson put it, to the "mushrooming" of secession sentiment. Northerners were riven in different ways, as the more progressive antislavery activists and abolitionists grew frustrated with any political move toward moderation and the maintenance of the status quo between free and slaveholding states.

When Abraham Lincoln, the Republican senator from Illinois, was elected president in 1860, the ideological die was cast. Little more than a month after Lincoln's election, South Carolina became the first state to secede from the Union. By early February 1861, six other states had joined South Carolina, and the Confederate States of America was formed with Mississippi senator Jefferson Davis as president. The following month, Lincoln stood at the Capitol and delivered his first inaugural address. In that speech, Lincoln affirmed the rights of southern states to maintain slavery and, going further, declared that he had "no purpose, directly or indirectly, to interfere with the institution of slavery." Lincoln did state, however, that the Union was insoluble and that his oath of office required that he protect the government and its possessions.

One such possession was Fort Sumter, an unfinished island fortification in the mouth of the Charleston Harbor. Union troops had garrisoned there shortly before Lincoln's inaugural address. Although the federal troops at Fort Sumter did not have the firepower or the supplies to be a tactical threat to the Confederacy, their presence was a sore point for southerners and soon the fort was surrounded. A military and political stalemate ensued, and a sustainable peace could not be achieved. Early in the morning on April 12, barely five weeks after Lincoln took office, Confederate troops fired upon Fort Sumter, thus starting the Civil War.

Fort Sumter, it bears noting, was one of two fortresses guarding the entrance to Charleston's harbor. The other was Fort Moultrie on Sullivan's Island, the entry point for almost half of the enslaved Africans who were brought to British North America and then the United States. Although the quarantine pesthouses at Sullivan's

Island had been out of use for decades by the time of southern secession, it is impossible to overstate the symbolic importance of these sites for the captured Africans who had disembarked here in order to be prepared for sale at slave markets. Charleston Harbor can be read as a place of multiple beginnings—few of them pleasant. It was the predominant North American port of entry for enslaved people, the direst site for the articulation of Confederate military power, and, one can argue, the starting point for a new meaning of citizenship for the Union and its loyalists.

Historians have been wrestling with Lincoln's views of African Americans and slavery since his presidency. He has been hailed as everything from the "Great Emancipator" to an unremitting racist who was cavalier in his use of derogatory language in regard to blacks. What is unambiguous, however, is that Lincoln was a pragmatist who was driven primarily by any idea that would contribute to preserving the Union. For example, at the start of the war, Lincoln proposed a plan of compensated emancipation, or paying slaveholders who freed their slaves. When that failed to attract support, Lincoln considered a colonization plan that would entail moving African Americans to Latin America. That idea, too, failed to take hold.

In part due to southern intransigence, Lincoln's views on slavery evolved. Even before war broke out, he was concerned primarily with slavery's social role and the effect it had on the possibility of national reconciliation. While he did not support slavery, he thought that it was impossible to eliminate it and preserve the Union.

Political and pragmatic pressures, however, led him to reconsider his views. That summer, as Lincoln began to think about how to secure a complete emancipation, he contemplated the military, economic, and political consequences of such a determined break with the original rationale for the war. In September 1862, Lincoln issued a preliminary emancipation proclamation. In this order,

Lincoln declared that all enslaved people in states still in rebellion on January 1, 1863, would become free on that day. Although the actual moment of federally directed emancipation was one hundred days away, the response was mixed.

The proclamation, like many political texts, demanded close reading. Most notably, it did not free enslaved people who lived in Delaware, Maryland, Kentucky, and Missouri, border states that were aligned with the Union. Further, slaveholders in the Confederacy were not about to abide by anything that Lincoln declared. Yet while the Emancipation Proclamation did little in a literal sense, its cultural and symbolic importance was monumental.

Was the Civil War about competing economic systems, political ideals, or philosophies concerning the sovereign rights of states versus those of the federal government? While these questions still prompt debate today, the Emancipation Proclamation made it clear to everyone that the war was, indeed, about slavery. Even if one began fighting for another reason—loyalty to a region or state, a culture, or a tradition—after the Emancipation Proclamation was issued, the question of slavery's preservation became the guiding issue in the Civil War.

One of Lincoln's worries related to the proclamation was the effect it would have on Union troop morale and enlistment. While Lincoln was correct to be concerned about a tide of resentment among northern soldiers who did not sign up to fight to end slavery, he underestimated the pent-up demand among African Americans to serve. After the Emancipation Proclamation took effect, that demand began to be addressed. (By the end of the war over 175,000 black men had served as soldiers in the Union Army, roughly 10 percent of the Union Army total.)

The Fifty-Fourth Massachusetts Volunteer Infantry was the first official African American regiment in the Civil War (others, all in the South, had been formed earlier but not with the endorsement of the federal government). It was organized one month after the Emancipation Proclamation took effect and was led by the white colonel Robert Gould Shaw of Boston. After a few months of training, the Fifty-Fourth sailed south to engage the enemy. There is little irony in the fact that it was called to action in South Carolina. More specifically, the regiment was charged with mounting an attack on Fort Wagner, a battlement that protected the southern approach to Charleston Harbor. In mid-July, six months after the proclamation reconfigured the scope and meaning of the Civil War, the Fifty-Fourth stormed Fort Wagner. The regiment was badly outmanned and outgunned, however, and almost half of the soldiers, including Colonel Shaw, died. Although unsuccessful in its bid to take over the stronghold, the Fifty-Fourth had its name etched in history, the bravery of the regiment serving as a powerful testament to African Americans' commitment to the Union and their desire to lay claim to the respect owed to a nation's citizens.

This commitment extended beyond those in uniform at the frontlines. African Americans also served in a range of jobs on supply lines, supporting troops in battle. Among them were black women, who worked as recruiters, nurses, cooks, laundry workers, and in more than a few instances, spies. Significantly, a lot of this African American labor was contributed by those who had been held in bondage. In this way, self-emancipated blacks became a great resource for Union armies. Their local knowledge of the southern terrain was invaluable, as was their willingness to provide the labor supporting the soldiers. At the same time, self-emancipated blacks presented a grave epidemiological challenge for Union armies, as they were often inadequately clothed, underfed, and in poor health. For these individuals, the pursuit of freedom and the dedication to its preservation were worth the risks associated with fleeing from slavery.

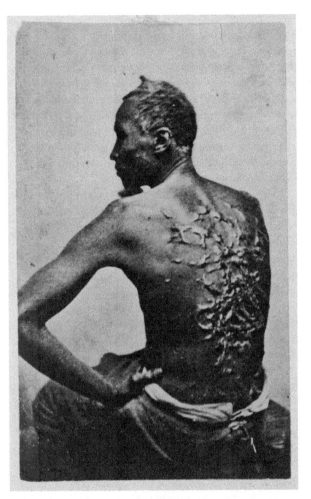

3. Gordon, an enslaved man who emancipated himself from a
Mississippi plantation in 1863, took refuge with the Union Army in
Baton Rouge, where his scars were discovered. This image, titled
The Scourged Back, was one of the first photographs to be used as
propaganda; as one contemporary newspaper remarked, "It tells the
story in a way that even Mrs. Stowe cannot approach, because it tells
the story to the eye."

Despite the heroics of African American soldiers like those in the Fifty-Fourth Infantry, Lincoln and the Union Army still struggled with securing enough troops to sustain the war effort. In the winter of 1863 Lincoln passed the Conscription Acts, which mandated military service for men ages twenty to forty-five (except those who could afford to pay $300 for an exemption). An unintended effect of the Conscription Acts was the exacerbation of class tensions within the Union. Coupled with the enormous death toll and the ambivalence that many white Americans felt about fighting for African American emancipation, these tensions neared a breaking point.

In the summer of 1863 they exploded into what became known as the New York City Draft Riots. Working-class Irish immigrants, who were regularly subject to virulent discrimination, played a crucial role in the port city as dockworkers. Though many lived alongside African Americans in the city, generally on peaceful terms, they felt threatened by the prospect of emancipated blacks moving north and competing for their jobs. Many were recent immigrants still struggling to establish themselves as American citizens, and that claim to citizenship rested in part on the fact that they were not black.

Following the first conscription lottery on July 11, 1863, mayhem ensued. Several days of riots ended only after military troops were brought in, and as many as one thousand people were killed. Rioters—mostly Irish and other white ethnic gangs—targeted those in uniform: soldiers, police, the region's military commandant. They also went after African Americans. Fights and beatings were pervasive, and even more horrifying, eleven people were lynched across the city. A seven-year-old boy, Joseph Reed, separated from his mother and grandmother, was beaten to death. Longshoremen assaulted a sailor, William Williams, and stabbed him before a crowd, chanting, "Don't hire niggers!" The Colored Orphanage was set on fire; thankfully, its occupants escaped. Abraham Franklin, a disabled black coachman, and his sister, Henrietta, were pulled out of their boarding room. Henrietta was beaten; Abraham was hanged. Federal troops, trying to quell the riot, cut down his body. As they departed, the rioting crowd hanged the body again and began chanting, "Jeff Davis!," invoking the president of the Confederacy. Later, a sixteen-year-old Irish butcher again cut down Abraham Franklin's body and dragged it through the streets as a trophy, linking his claim to citizenship to the corpse of a disabled black man.

After his reelection in November 1864, Lincoln initiated plans to complete emancipation. Concerned that after the war there might be attempts to interpret the Emancipation Proclamation as a wartime resolution rather than a permanent one, he began working with Congress for the passage of what would become the Thirteenth Amendment to the Constitution. Ratified in 1865, the amendment abolished slavery definitively. (It was the first of three so-called Reconstruction Amendments. The Fourteenth Amendment [1868] established the lines of citizenship and guaranteed due process. The Fifteenth Amendment [1870] guaranteed that the right to vote would not be denied on the basis of race or previous servitude.)

By the late winter of 1865, the Union forces had the clear upper hand and a northern victory was imminent. Along with moving the nation toward full emancipation, Lincoln had already offered a plan on how to reconstruct the Union after the war's conclusion. His first effort in this regard was a "Ten Percent Plan." It involved granting a pardon to all southerners (except Confederate leaders) who took an oath of loyalty to the Union and supported emancipation. Once 10 percent of a state's white male population signed the oath, a new government could be formed. Antislavery activists, congressional radicals, and staunch Union supporters found the plan far too lenient. But Lincoln never had the chance to advance a new reconstruction plan. On April 14, 1865, Confederate loyalist John Wilkes Booth walked up behind the president while he was enjoying a play in Ford's Theatre and shot him in the head. Lincoln would die the next day.

Following Lincoln's assassination, Andrew Johnson took office and developed a series of measures known as Presidential Reconstruction. Like Lincoln, Johnson sought to extend a pardon to most white southerners, but he excluded both Confederate leaders and wealthy planters. Johnson believed that moneyed landowners were the source of many of the South's problems and that they should not be in charge as the region set up postslavery governments.

Republicans in Congress were horrified by Johnson's approach. They fought him at every turn. Against southern protestations, the Republican-controlled Congress ushered in a series of reforms that became known as Radical or Congressional Reconstruction. Beginning in 1867, the South was divided into five military districts controlled by northern and Republican governments and occupied by federal troops.

Although driven by competing philosophies about how to secure a just and lasting peace, the architects of Presidential Reconstruction and then Radical Reconstruction shared the desire to heal the Union quickly. The daily uncertainties bred by war may have been receding, but they were being replaced by many more questions about what a reconstructed nation might look like. Questions related to political autonomy, the nature of labor, and free will played central roles in the era. White southerners, in particular, eagerly sought answers. They wondered what to do with emancipated African Americans, how to control them, and how or if the South would survive the social, cultural, and economic upheaval.

Southern white anxiety about these issues was well founded. On the electoral front, the pace of change in southern society was beyond their worst fears. In 1870 Congress ratified the Fifteenth

Amendment, guaranteeing African American men the right to vote. Blacks took immediate advantage of the opportunity, and there was a subsequent dramatic increase in the number of African Americans holding elected office. Black men began to win elections to town councils or as local sheriffs, as well as to positions in state and federal governments. Within a few years, African American men from eight former Confederate states were serving in Congress.

For African Americans, the end of slavery meant liberation. For white slaveholders, including both plantation owners and members of small slaveholding households, it meant a loss of wealth and labor. For blacks and whites, it meant an immediate, profound instability in the social fabric.

While southerners began to assess the economic devastation of the war, white planters were eager to return to plantation labor to get their crops planted and harvested. African Americans were eager to earn money, but they also sought economic autonomy, particularly via landownership. White landowners wanted blacks to sign labor contracts to work on their farms, but blacks rejected this notion; they expected the federal government to help redistribute southern land. Very quickly, state laws interceded that answered the question of what to do with the newly free African American population. These so-called black codes differed from state to state, but collectively created a new social and economic system that, upon closer inspection, looked uncomfortably familiar to African Americans.

Some black codes permitted African Americans to acquire property, marry, make contracts, sue and be sued, and testify in court against other African Americans—all impossible under slavery. But although the black codes appeared to afford citizenship rights, they were ultimately geared toward labor stabilization. Some states required African Americans to show proof of annual labor contracts, which meant remaining at a job for an entire year. Ordinary white citizens were empowered to arrest African Americans who seemed to be breaking such contracts.

Other codes stated that African Americans could not "steal labor" without risking an exorbitant $500 fine. Stealing labor could be interpreted as not working hard enough or as saving something for oneself when working on white-owned land. In some states, blacks were prohibited from renting land in urban areas—an effort to prevent critical masses of African Americans from developing economic autonomy. Black codes prohibited African Americans from hunting or owning weapons. They also regulated social behavior: preventing black women from entering public spaces, forbidding certain styles of dress, and enacting curfews. The codes addressed vagrancy, idleness, rude gestures, mischief, and preaching the gospel without a license. Their vagueness made it easy for lawmakers to punish supposed violations with fines or involuntary plantation labor. And speaking of labor, black codes forced African American minors, primarily orphans and the children of poor parents, to work without wages in apprenticeships.

These wide-ranging laws were often plainly unjustifiable. Fairly soon after they were established, sometimes within months, many black codes were declared illegal and eliminated.

In place of the black codes, a new system developed that was focused more explicitly upon labor: sharecropping. Sharecropping revolved around credit. White farm owners, who owned land, tools, and seed, required African American laborers to rent their equipment and property at an exorbitantly priced company store. The laborers would repay their debt via their shares of the crop they harvested. Inevitably, when white landowners brought the crop to market (without sharecroppers present), they would return to the farm bemoaning low commodity prices and declaring that sharecroppers still owed them money. Sharecroppers were stuck, required to keep working in order to eliminate their debt. The cycle repeated. Even if African Americans were no longer being whipped by overseers, they remained in perpetual, inescapable servitude. Sharecropping began in the mid-1860s and remained prevalent throughout the South until the 1940s. Only the systematic mechanization of farms ultimately broke the cycle.

Both the black codes and the sharecropping system aimed to recreate slavery with a different name and slightly different nature. Through draconian restrictions on behavior and cycles of debt, whites asserted economic and social control over African Americans. But within the limited range of their own opportunities, African Americans remained undeterred and continued to seek an education, secure land, and gain access to the ballot box. Further, they believed that the federal government would help them attain full citizenship rights and property ownership.

Part of this expectation grew from the federal military presence throughout the South, but African Americans had other reasons to look toward the federal government for intervention and a measure of justice. For many African Americans—and for many poor whites as well—the most tangible federal intervention came in the form of the Bureau of Freed Refugees, Freedmen, and Abandoned Lands, better known as the Freedmen's Bureau.

Established in March 1865, the Freedmen's Bureau was tasked with providing food, shelter, and medical aid to the destitute, both black and white. The South, predominantly an agricultural economy before the start of the war, lagged behind the North in terms of mechanized industry, infrastructure, healthcare, and education. The southern economy and infrastructure were decimated in the war, and the region was beset with systemic epidemiological challenges as large swaths of its population lacked access to proper clothing, shelter, and food. In his book *Sick from Freedom*, Jim Downs paints a bleak picture in which hundreds of thousands of emancipated African Americans suffered from exposure to the elements and from diseases like yellow fever and smallpox. Downs writes that tens of thousands became sick and died in what he terms "the largest biological crisis of the nineteenth century."

In addition to addressing this health crisis, the Freedmen's Bureau was responsible for providing education to freed people. Furthermore, the bureau aimed to establish free labor arrangements in former plantation areas with the goal of developing an economic system in which African Americans could retain autonomy as they signed labor contracts. Finally, the bureau was charged with securing justice for blacks in legal proceedings.

The bureau's record was mixed at best. At one point, it controlled 850,000 acres of property that, instead of being transferred to poor whites and to blacks, were returned to their original owners. Its attempt to establish wage labor contracts—under which African Americans could escape the sharecropping system—failed. It did succeed, remarkably, in establishing schools. From 1865 to 1869, three hundred thousand new schools for blacks were established. These schools were not on par with white schools, but their very existence was a shocking change. By 1872, however, the bureau closed when Congress refused to extend its authorization. The bureau's funding had already been slashed in previous years, and bureau officials on the ground had been increasingly harassed by new white supremacist groups that bristled at the larger agenda of educating African Americans, redistributing wealth, and supporting African American claims on citizenship.

The most important and assertive of these groups was the Ku Klux Klan, established in Tennessee in 1866. Given the strictures placed on African Americans by the slave economy, a group like the Klan was unnecessary prior to emancipation. In the

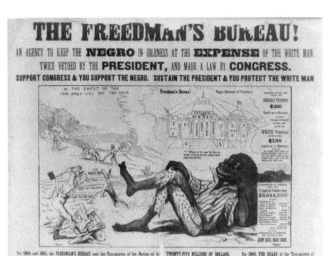

4. Created in support of a white supremacist gubernatorial candidate in an 1866 Pennsylvania election, this racist political broadside takes aim at Radical Republicans' support of the Freedman's Bureau by means of a grotesque caricature, which depicts a lazy black freedman—"Whar is de use for me to work as long as dey make dese appropriations," he muses—surrounded by images of hardworking white men.

postbellum South, however, white anxiety about the consequences of African American freedom and a burgeoning white resentment about the remaking of their social and cultural fabric created a perfect environment for a group like the KKK to emerge. For many whites, the Klan represented a declaration that a southern way of life would be preserved. To that end, the Klan targeted African Americans (as well as outsiders like northern politicians, Jews, and Catholics). Klan members burned black-owned property, threatened those who tried to vote, terrorized black women through sexual violence, and assaulted black men and women who "forgot their place."

Much like the record of the Freedmen's Bureau, the larger record of Radical Reconstruction was mixed. Despite the many challenges that African Americans faced, they still made tremendous strides in the postbellum era. The pace of positive change only increased during Radical Reconstruction. But with those positive developments came a rising tide of white southern resistance. And though the federal military quickly addressed the challenges that the Klan presented (by temporarily eradicating the group in the early 1870s), the North was weary of southern intransigence and resistance. For their part, white southerners were tired of the northern presence and angry about new state constitutions written under Republican-controlled governments that they believed afforded too many rights to African American men. If the architects of Radical Reconstruction believed that they could forcibly knit the Union back together, they underestimated the intensity with which white southerners clung to their way of life. A national exhaustion driven by these battles over Reconstruction politics had set in.

In the 1876 presidential election, Democrat Samuel Tilden won the popular vote, beating Republican Rutherford B. Hayes. The electoral vote was unclear due to contested results in southern states. Politicians brokered a deal known as the Compromise of 1877. Hayes was granted the presidency; in exchange, the federal government pulled northern troops out of the South, giving the South the chance to reorganize itself within the Union. With this compromise, a period of incredible possibility, complicated reality, growing white southern intransigence, and uncertainty among white northerners came to a close.

In less than twenty years, the nation had gone to war with itself, slavery was abolished, and a series of constitutional amendments were ratified that clarified who could be a citizen, asserted the importance of due process in legal matters, and expanded the right to vote to include African American men. The South failed to preserve its economic system, lost the wealth embodied in enslaved African Americans, and had to establish a new understanding of what labor could look like, what freedom meant, and who could be a citizen.

The ideological battle over all of these things, however, was just beginning. A major theme in the history of the post–Civil War United States is the struggle over how this moment is remembered. Cultural symbols from the Civil War era remain powerfully relevant today. Most visible is the Confederate battle flag, which appears on license plates and a vast amount of merchandise and, until July 2020, could still be found on the state flag of Mississippi. Those who deploy the battle flag claim that it is a symbol of tradition and heritage; others see it as a manifestation of racist violence and degradation. Similarly, debates about how the era is memorialized circulate around statuary and memorials to Confederate leaders or the honoring of Confederates and their allies by naming streets and buildings after them. These debates, regrettably, have lingered in the nation's education system, with pitched battles over "which" history is taught and how.

Chapter 4
Civilization, race, and the politics of uplift

> Southern trees bear strange fruit,
> Blood on the leaves and blood at the root,
> Black bodies swinging in the southern breeze,
> Strange fruit hanging from the poplar trees.

This excerpt from "Strange Fruit," made famous by blues singer Billie Holiday, requires little elaboration. Written in 1937 by Abel Meeropol in recognition of the resurgence of racial violence in the early twentieth century, "Strange Fruit" offers a cutting commentary on the risks associated with being African American in the United States. It effectively captures the abiding threat of the post–Civil War rise of white supremacist logic that declared that African Americans were uncivilized and unprepared for the rigors of citizenship. Despite the persistent threat of violence, African Americans pushed back with determination, creating their own institutions within the confines of an increasingly segregated country, engaging in their own debates about the best path forward toward full citizenship, and embracing new sensibilities about race pride, potential, and progress.

This new phase of African American life in the United States was marked by the end of the federal occupation of the South in 1877 and the end of Reconstruction. The era immediately following Reconstruction became known as Redemption because it involved whites' attempts to reclaim what they thought had been under attack during Reconstruction. Their South needed to be redeemed.

As Republican governments faded with the departure of federal troops, southerners worked to restore white power. The KKK, which had been wiped out by the military soon after its founding, reemerged with a vengeance. Other means of asserting white control were developed. The most effective of these were clearly in evidence when it came to the voting booth.

A range of tactics to limit African American voting power quickly emerged during Redemption: gerrymandering (the reconfiguration of districts to negate the effect of black votes), poll taxes (which required proof of payment on land taxes—something you could not supply if you did not own land), grandfather clauses (which limited voting to those men whose grandfathers had voted, thereby excluding African Americans), and literacy tests (which involved onerous requirements like reciting part of the state constitution from memory).

If those limiting maneuvers weren't enough, white actors deployed other tactics to cut off access to the vote. In some southern areas it became clear that just registering to vote could be a matter of life or death. Those African American men who managed to register still had to navigate the challenge of actually voting. It was not uncommon for black voters to find someone standing outside the voting booth with a whip, threatening those who voted Republican. The people doing this dirty work were often members of local militias like the Klan. Finally, if all the aforementioned methods of voter suppression failed, there was always the ultimate form of racial harassment: lynching.

Lynching was rare prior to the Civil War because to lynch an enslaved person was to destroy somebody's property. During Reconstruction, federal military presence mitigated this violence, but once that presence was gone, lynching became a way that the

South redeemed itself. Between 1882 and 1901, more than one hundred lynchings per year were recorded nationally, the great majority of them in the South. Between 1882 and 1968, more than five thousand people died in lynchings; at least three-quarters were African American. These statistics represent only recorded lynchings, and actual numbers continue to be revised higher as historians uncover new records of this type of violence.

Lynchings ranged in scope and method. Most happened under the cover of night and were perpetrated by small groups determined to exact justice on their terms. Some were public and well-documented grotesqueries that were advertised in the local paper. Professional photographers frequently documented the horror, only to amplify it when they sold the reproductions as prints and postcards.

It was not unusual for victims to be physically assaulted and mutilated while still conscious before being hanged or tied to a post to be burned alive. Even after the lynching, the abuse to the body might not end. Scholar and activist W. E. B. Du Bois recounted being in Atlanta in 1899 after Sam Hose was lynched. Du Bois was headed to the editorial offices of the *Atlanta Constitution* to talk about this lynching when he learned that parts of Hose's body had been cut off and were for sale as souvenirs in a nearby store. The inhumanity of the moment never left Du Bois's consciousness.

Like Sam Hose, the majority of lynch victims were African American men accused of rape. The presumption was that a black man who raped a white woman had also violated the sanctity of the South. Typically, language around lynching framed it as a manly act: black brutes were uncivilized rapists, and lynch mobs were protectors of white women and civilization. As historian Gail Bederman has shown, deploying the concept of being civilized was a strategic choice in this era. As the United States was rapidly industrializing, being "civilized" became a way to exercise control in a landscape of changing cultural values. Being civilized, or declaring another group uncivilized, was a way of marking one's place in the world.

Ida B. Wells, a black female journalist and civil rights pioneer, tapped into this logic but turned it against itself. Based in Memphis, Tennessee, Wells became an anti-lynching activist after a friend, Thomas Moss, was murdered for opening a store that competed with a nearby white-owned business. Outraged by the injustice, Wells organized boycotts and wrote editorials that excoriated this unabashed racial violence. When she argued that lynching was a manifestation of uncivilized white male behavior, Wells shocked her audiences by turning widespread ideas about race and civilization upside down. Wells further upset common beliefs when her investigations of lynching across the country revealed that in many cases lynch victims were not even accused of rape, but rather theft, rudeness, or assault. Thomas Moss was lynched merely for introducing economic competition into a community. Wells's editorials and speeches had personal consequences. After she wrote that some white women resorted to claims of rape to cover up their desire for African American men, Wells had to flee Memphis. She would never return.

Against this backdrop of violence and ideology, other African American reformers were hard at work, determined to improve the life chances of poor blacks. Much of this work flowed through churches, societies, and associations whose members envisioned and fought for communal, long-term gains. These reformers saw it as their duty to uplift the race.

The notion of "uplift" was simultaneously subversive and conservative. At its core, it was an ideology committed to improving the quality of African American life that also aligned with the restrictive gender and class conventions of its era. Its roots can be traced to the American Baptist Home Mission Society, a northern, white-run effort to educate southern African

Americans. Its leaders included Henry Morehouse, a white man who coined the phrase "talented tenth" to suggest that 10 percent of black America would uplift the race as a whole.

The politics of such organizations were fraught. Black religious activity during this era was in flux, as organized religious bodies clashed with grassroots worship. Some African Americans were suspicious of groups like the Home Mission Society, whose white northern members aimed to civilize African Americans through Christian ethics. In 1895 a group of southern blacks, frustrated by the American Baptist Home Mission Society's edicts, formed their own society, the National Baptist Convention. Created by and for black people, the convention rejected white society's patronizing attitudes and aimed to establish African American control over black churches, religious practices, and secular activities.

Aligned with this push to uplift the race were various secular black organizations. In 1896 one of the more prominent of these organizations emerged: the National Association of Colored Women (NACW). The NACW's motto was "Lifting while we climb." Its members were middle- and upper-class black women who organized campaigns and protests in support of various causes. For example, in an era when cities were hotbeds of disease, NACW members taught proper hygiene to poor black urban residents and waged anti-tuberculosis campaigns. The NACW also engaged in explicit acts of political resistance, like picketing and lobbying in support of anti-lynching legislation. Although its goals were progressive, the organization also had a conservative outlook in that its members considered it their duty to teach lower-class African Americans how to behave respectably. For the women of the NAWC, uplift was a manifestation of the Victorian sense of white middle-class propriety they had grown up with, and they felt they had a special duty to save the race.

Anna Julia Cooper, an educator and the leading black feminist theorist of her day, exemplified the uplift ideology espoused by the

NACW. After a successful career as an educator at M Street High School in Washington, DC, the nation's best black public high school, Cooper pursued graduate studies at the Sorbonne, receiving her doctorate when she was sixty-three. Upon returning to the United States, she established Frelinghuysen University, an institution that provided evening classes for black workers who wanted to improve their employment prospects.

In 1892, while teaching at M Street, Cooper published *A Voice from the South*. In a key passage, she wrote, "Only the black woman can say where and when I enter, in the quiet, undisputed dignity of my womanhood, without violence and without suing or special patronage, then and there the whole Negro race enters with me." African American women, Cooper declared, could say how, when, and where blacks would join society as rightful members. This was the epitome of uplift ideology with all of its best and complicated social biases.

Uplift ideology was not limited to the women's sphere. Leading black male activists with starkly different political strategies for securing African American freedom argued over the best way to save the race. The most enduring of these debates revolved around accommodation and assimilation, typically represented by Booker T. Washington and W. E. B. Du Bois, respectively.

Born enslaved in 1856, Washington worked in the West Virginia coalfields before and after emancipation. His college training at Hampton Institute focused on vocational education and technical expertise rather than high culture or the liberal arts. This pedagogy made a deep impression on Washington. In 1881 he established the Tuskegee Institute. Located in the town of Tuskegee, Alabama, in the heart of white farming country, the institute succeeded because of Washington's skill at building coalitions that ostensibly crossed racial lines and class boundaries while also respecting both. Although Tuskegee was not a racial oasis or a site of full social integration, the school eventually became the town's

5. Born into slavery in Raleigh, North Carolina, Anna Julia Cooper became a pathbreaking black feminist intellectual and educator. In this portrait she poses next to a bust of Frederick Douglass in the offices of Frelinghuysen University, a school for black workers where she served as president from 1930 to 1941.

lifeblood and economic engine. As such, it became a manifestation of Washington's long-term strategy: through slow, hard work, African Americans would become so economically vital that whites could not help but incorporate them into society.

Washington's go-slow approach, combined with his ability to interact with white business leaders, made him the darling of philanthropists. These individuals were attracted to Washington's work largely out of self-interest: they believed that Washington was training a smart, technically adept workforce of docile, second-class citizens. Northern business interests, in particular, donated substantial amounts of money to him.

In 1895 Washington's ascent accelerated with his address to the Atlanta Cotton Exposition. In that speech he called on white employers to recognize blacks' native loyalty, but he also exhorted blacks to be patient in their desire for progress. Washington said, "To those of my race who depend on bettering their condition in a foreign land or who underestimate the importance of cultivating friendly relations with the southern white man, who is their next-door neighbor, I would say: 'Cast down your bucket where you are'—cast it down in making friends in every manly way of the people of all races by whom we are surrounded." He continued, "The wisest among our race understand that the agitation of questions of social equality is the extremest folly." Elaborating, he noted, "In all things that are purely social, we can be as separate as the fingers; yet one as the hand in all things essential to mutual progress."

Between 1895 and his death in 1915, Washington became the most powerful African American in the country, in part because his approach to race management aligned with the emerging legal consensus about the mixing of the races. After the Civil War, state legislatures began to issue laws designed to separate the races. By the mid-1870s, these "Jim Crow" laws regulated public accommodation and transportation. The newly entrenched system pervaded virtually every facet of daily life.

In 1896 the Supreme Court issued the landmark decision *Plessy v. Ferguson*. The case involved a Louisiana man, Homer Plessy, who bought a rail ticket in 1892. After Plessy took a seat in the whites-only first-class coach and refused to move, he was jailed for breaking a Jim Crow statute. Plessy's action was intentional: he wanted to challenge segregation laws and assumed he would be successful. Plessy argued that segregation violated the Thirteenth and Fourteenth Amendments of the Constitution. The Supreme Court disagreed. In an 8–1 decision, the Court held: "We consider the underlying fallacy of the plaintiff's argument to consist in the assumption that the enforced separation of the races stamps the colored race with a badge of inferiority. If this be so, it is not by reason of anything found in the act, but solely because the colored race chooses to put that construction on it." In a dissent, Justice John Harlan wrote that "the arbitrary separation of the citizens on the basis of race, while they are on a public highway, is a badge of servitude, wholly inconsistent with the civil freedom and the equality before the law established by the Constitution." While Harlan's dissent would eventually become a guiding legal principle, his was a lonely voice on the Court. *Plessy* remained the law of the land for nearly sixty years.

It is easy to condemn Washington from the convenience of the present, but it is worth considering what was possible for an African American leader in the Deep South. Washington worked in an environment where lynching was omnipresent and the black vote had virtually disappeared. Fully 75 percent of African Americans lived in the former Confederate South. Approximately 50 percent of the southern population was black, but blacks owned just over 10 percent of the farms. Outside of institutes like Tuskegee, there were few schools that offered an agricultural education, and farm production was low. In effect, the southern black population was politically, socially, and economically aggrieved and lived in a state of racial terror. In this context, pursuing economic independence prior to fighting for rights was not an unreasonable strategy.

Yet it was not the only option. Du Bois offered an alternative. (Anna Julia Cooper anticipated many of Du Bois's ideas in *A Voice from the South*, but her contributions on this topic have often been obscured.) In a memorable critique of Washington, Du Bois wrote, "Manly self-respect is worth more than lands and houses, and a people who voluntarily surrender such respect, or cease striving for it, are not worth civilizing." He rejected Washington's call to relinquish political power, instead insisting on civil rights and advocating for the education of the talented tenth.

This agenda reflected Du Bois's experience. Born in 1868 in Great Barrington, Massachusetts, he attended Fisk University, studied in Berlin, and received a PhD from Harvard. Du Bois created the field of urban sociology with his 1898 book *The Philadelphia Negro* and taught at Atlanta University, where he edited a long series of studies of social problems, doing what he could to connect theory, practice, and social reform.

In his 1903 book, *The Souls of Black Folk*, Du Bois offered a stinging critique of Washington's accommodationism. In a chapter titled "Of Mr. Booker T. Washington and Others," Du Bois argued that the "thinking classes of American Negroes" carried a special burden. They had "a responsibility to themselves, a responsibility to the struggling masses, a responsibility to the darker races of men whose future depends so largely on this American experiment, but especially a responsibility to this nation." He argued that Washington's ideology led to "industrial slavery and civic death."

Washington's and Du Bois's ideologies came into direct conflict in 1905 when Du Bois and other black professionals, including Ida B. Wells, met at Niagara Falls to form an organization dedicated to full citizenship rights for black Americans. Known as the Niagara Movement, the group demanded freedom of speech, full citizenship, male suffrage, the abolition of racial distinctions, and respect for working people. Washington was invited to join but declined to participate, unwilling to risk alienating his white support base.

In 1909 members of the Niagara Movement were asked to attend a national conference on race relations and civil rights. The event was led by white activists, many from abolitionist families, in response to a 1908 race riot and lynching in Springfield, Illinois. The riot began when a white woman accused an African American worker of assaulting and raping her. She later recanted, but it was too late. Mobs attacked African Americans suspected of harboring the accused rapist. The riot occurred on the centennial of Abraham Lincoln's birth, and black citizens were lynched near Lincoln's home and gravesite. That the Great Emancipator's memory could be so sullied horrified these white liberals. With a few Niagara Movement representatives, they formed a new organization dedicated to African American civil rights, the National Association for the Advancement of Colored People (NAACP).

Du Bois became the NAACP's director of research and publicity and editor of its magazine, the *Crisis*. At its founding and for many years after, he was the sole African American officer. The NAACP focused primarily on legal and intellectual work, and its leaders prioritized assimilation. African Americans, they believed, eventually would integrate into white society—and not vice versa. Other organizations also worked to improve black life via different strategies. Most prominent was the National Urban League, founded in 1911, which focused on finding jobs for African American migrants. The Urban League's work, in particular, came at a critical time.

At the turn of the twentieth century black America was overwhelmingly a rural, southern population. That changed as massive numbers of African Americans moved north in the so-called Great Migration, at the time the greatest internal migration in US history. The Great Migration has to be understood as both a demographic shift and a political movement. African Americans with the resources to migrate did so because the political gains of Reconstruction had been systematically stripped away. Their ability to vote had disappeared, state-funded education had become functionally nonexistent, social segregation was increasing, the threat of lynching loomed, and the sharecropping system forced farmers into second-class citizenship and dead-end employment that looked too much like slavery.

Various factors amplified the scale of the Great Migration. Chief among them was the abundance of jobs in the North. Labor agents, employed by the owners of mines, factories, and mills, abetted this process. They traveled south and spoke glowingly of northern life to rural black workers, even offering to pay their train fare north. The *Chicago Defender*, the era's most important African American newspaper, also played an important role in the relocation. The *Defender* circulated broadly throughout the South and encouraged migration by featuring letters to the editor relaying opportunities available in the North and regularly detailing the horrors of southern lynchings.

In the North, black migrants found a mixed quality of life. Housing was de facto segregated, often poorly maintained, and located in high-crime neighborhoods rife with public health hazards. Migrants frequently encountered hostility from northern blacks who had been there for generations and held the new arrivals in disregard for their dress, customs, and dialect. The new arrivals' treatment suffered further because their presence increased the competition for jobs. Even as the Urban League devoted significant resources to helping African American migrants, some of the organization's tactics provided short-term gains that damaged long-term relationships. For example, the Urban League would collaborate with factory owners when their unionized white workers went on strike, securing African Americans as scab laborers, who in turn were vilified by striking workers.

As the Great Migration destabilized southern society, white resistance became increasingly palpable. Its most obvious manifestation was the KKK. Destroyed at the national level during Reconstruction, the Klan crept back during Redemption, and its popularity skyrocketed around 1915, just as the Great Migration reached its peak. This was not a coincidence.

Much of the Klan's resurgent popularity can be attributed to D. W. Griffith's film *The Birth of a Nation* (1915). Based on Thomas Dixon's novel *The Clansman*, the film depicted Reconstruction from an explicitly racist point of view. In its climactic scenes, a newly freed man (a white actor in blackface makeup) stalks a white woman, who avoids being raped only by leaping off a cliff. She dies in her brother's arms, and he retaliates by lynching her assailant and organizing the Klan in an attempt to maintain social control, protect white womanhood, and redeem the South.

The Birth of a Nation was a runaway hit. It played to sold-out audiences around the country, earning over $10 million in its first release. It also earned the ire of the NAACP, which issued a forty-seven-page pamphlet titled "Fighting a Vicious Film: Protest against 'The Birth of the Nation,'" held rallies at theaters, and famously referred to it as "three miles of filth." Griffith's film opened conversations about the promise of the American ideal, inviting its supporters to lament their forced sacrifices in the age of dawning black freedom. To its detractors, the movie was further evidence of a long-broken promise.

In 1918, with *The Birth of a Nation* still in the public's mind and sixteen months after the United States entered World War I, Du Bois wrote an editorial for the *Crisis* called "Close Ranks," in which he called for African Americans to have faith in the nation's democratic promise: "Let us, while this war lasts, forget our special grievances and close our ranks shoulder to shoulder with our own white fellow citizens and the allied nations that are fighting for democracy." Du Bois argued that by enlisting, African Americans would earn respect that would translate into civil rights after the war. In an era of continuing racial violence, "Close

Ranks" angered many black leaders because it admonished blacks to forget their "special grievances."

Those grievances took different forms in the North and Midwest than in the South. African American migrants often burdened social service agencies, destabilized the housing market, and exacerbated labor tensions, forming a powder keg that could explode into violence. The East St. Louis riots offer a stark example. On July 2, 1917, striking white workers in local aluminum factories were furious when they were replaced by black scab workers. They started fights that turned into citywide violence. The police looked the other way as dozens of African American citizens were murdered and thousands of black families were left homeless. In response, the NAACP organized a silent march down New York City's Fifth Avenue. Led by muffled drums, ten thousand men, women, and children marched from Harlem to the heart of Manhattan in dead silence, carrying banners that read, "Mr. President, why not make America safe for democracy?" and "Mother, do lynchers go to heaven?" Two years later the marchers received mixed messages in response.

The summer of 1919 is known as the Red Summer, a name evoking the blood that was shed in race riots in twenty-five midwestern and northern cities. The worst riots took place in Chicago in July when Eugene Williams, a young African American boy floating in Lake Michigan, strayed over an unmarked line at a segregated beach. Williams was stoned from the shore and drowned. As news of the murder swept across Chicago, white ethnic street gangs—already angered by housing tensions that had emerged as African American migrants moved into previously white neighborhoods—roved about with the stated purpose of defending their turf. In the ensuing five-day riot, roughly forty people (most African American) were killed, and five thousand were injured. Much as in East St. Louis, police stood by and let white mobs attack. Peace returned only when the Illinois National

Guard arrived. Unlike their counterparts in East St. Louis, black Chicagoans responded with militancy, forcefully defending their neighborhoods.

That change in attitude can be understood in a broader sociopolitical context. Around three hundred thousand African Americans fought in World War I. After serving admirably in Europe—and being treated like heroes by locals in England and France—the soldiers returned home expecting justice and full citizenship. Briefly, progress seemed possible. When the 369th Infantry Regiment, known as the Hellfighters, returned in 1919, one million people watched them parade from Lower Manhattan to Harlem. Marching in the opposite direction as had the participants in the NAACP's silent protest, they received a hero's welcome.

Yet early optimism proved premature. After several years of decline, lynchings skyrocketed in 1919. Of the eighty-plus lynchings recorded that year, at least ten targeted returning soldiers, most murdered while in uniform. This was social control at its most grotesque. Du Bois realized his grave error in the previous year's editorial, and in a new column, "Returning Soldiers," he wrote: "This country of ours, despite all its better souls have done and dreamed, is yet a shameful land. It lynches. It disfranchises its own citizens. It encourages ignorance. It steals from us. It insults us. This is the country to which we, soldiers of democracy, return.... We return. We return from fighting. We return fighting."

The editorial captured a pervasive mentality among African Americans. Black urban residents were fed up with the racial violence that plagued cities. Across the United States, African Americans still suffered terrible discrimination and had difficulty securing jobs or decent housing. The shocking news of African American soldiers lynched in uniform, coupled with the anger recently voiced by leaders like Du Bois, conveyed the sense that a new political climate had emerged, one in which blacks would insist on having their civil rights—or else.

Although state governments, particularly southern ones, had a well-established history of placing barriers before their black subjects, African Americans' growing insistence on securing full citizenship did not go unnoticed by the federal government. After World War I, federal surveillance of African Americans grew sharply. The riots of 1917 and 1919 unsettled white politicians, including a young J. Edgar Hoover. In 1919 Hoover became head of the Department of Justice's new General Intelligence Division. He investigated "liberal activity," an intentionally vague construct that Hoover leaned on to rationalize infiltrating African American groups across the political spectrum.

Under Hoover's leadership, a prime early target of surveillance was Marcus Garvey. Born in Jamaica in 1887, Garvey was educated in London. Upon returning to Jamaica in 1914, he organized the Universal Negro Improvement Association (UNIA). Inspired by Booker T. Washington's notion of economic self-sufficiency, Garvey aspired to emancipate blacks across the globe through economic empowerment and empire formation. As he wrote in his Declaration of Rights of the Negro Peoples of the World (1920), "We believe in the freedom of Africa for the Negro people of the world, and by the principle of Europe for the Europeans and Asia for the Asiatics, we also demand Africa for the Africans at home and abroad."

In 1916 Garvey moved to Harlem. He published a popular journal, *Negro World*, which served as the mouthpiece for his nationalist philosophy of racial pride and unity. Garvey's reputation blossomed, and he soon claimed to have six million followers. There is little doubt that his popularity was connected to his vision: "We have outgrown slavery, but our minds are still enslaved to the thinking of the master race. Now take those kinks out of your mind instead of out of your hair.... We have a beautiful history and we shall create another one in the future." When African Americans realized their potential, Garvey believed, they would rise up and anoint him as their leader. In preparation for that moment, Garvey organized parades in which uniformed UNIA members marched in front of him while, in his convertible, Garvey presented himself as a benevolent emperor, bedecked with epaulets, gold buttons, trim, and plumage.

Garvey's plans ranged from the realistic to the absurd. If the UNIA laundries, groceries, and other retail operations were the most practical expression of his ideology, the Black Star Steamship Line, launched in 1919, was the most fantastical. Given the enormity of Garvey's ambitions, the Black Star became the crown jewel of his efforts: a steamship line that would demonstrate black self-sufficiency and nation-building potential. Garvey began selling bonds to raise money for ships that would exemplify black power as they employed all-black crews, took African Americans to Africa, and became a linchpin of the global economy. Initially promising, the project quickly became Garvey's undoing. While the few ships he was able to secure became powerful symbols of possibility, the enterprise became a business and legal fiasco.

Garvey's mass popularity, appeals for race pride, and haughty imperialist style worried people like Hoover. In 1923 Hoover indicted Garvey on mail fraud charges related to the Black Star Line, and in 1925 the head of the UNIA was sentenced to five years in prison. Before Garvey's term could be completed, he was pardoned by President Coolidge on the condition that he return to Jamaica and never return. Garvey accepted the stipulation and was deported in 1927.

The year Garvey was sentenced to prison, Howard University philosopher Alain Locke edited a special issue of the journal *Survey Graphic*. That journal captured the spirit of a new cultural mentality that was being expressed by African Americans throughout the country. The special edition included poetry, essays, excerpts from plays, and short stories. Locke added material to the edition to produce a book, *The New Negro*, published in 1926. That book became the bible for this new artistic moment, typically referred to as the Harlem, or New Negro, Renaissance.

Most historians point to African American soldiers' return in 1919 as the movement's beginning. There is no consensus about when the movement ended. What there is little debate about, however, is the importance of the New Negro Renaissance as a barometer of a shifted African American cultural sensibility that grew directly out of the dislocations associated with the Great Migration as well as the heightened racial awareness and political impatience that arose after World War I.

While mostly articulated as a moment of cultural discovery, Locke saw the Renaissance as a political movement shrouded in the cloth of culture. Further, he understood culture itself as a political battleground. He believed the Renaissance was a fight for cultural recognition that, once gained, would prove that African Americans deserved freedom and equality. In his introduction to *The New Negro*, Locke wrote, "For the younger generation is vibrant with a new psychology; the new spirit is awake in the masses, and under the very eyes of the professional observers is transforming what has been a perennial problem into the progressive phases of contemporary Negro life."

Although Locke saw culture as a means toward a political end, he also had an expansive view of culture. Unlike the talented tenth leaders who preceded him, Locke found much to praise in the folk culture that was most often connected to the black experience. He was not alone in this: Renaissance artists like poet Sterling A. Brown (*Southern Road*) and cultural anthropologist Zora Neale Hurston (*Mules and Men* and *Their Eyes Were Watching God*) hailed folk heritage, viewing it as the authentic depiction of a rich and complex black life. Editor and novelist Jessie Fauset (*There Is Confusion* and *Plum Bun*) also sought to portray black life in all of its honesty. Unlike Brown's and Hurston's orientation, however, Fauset focused on upper-class African Americans, even when doing so raised other, painful issues like intraracial class politics and racial passing.

Celebrations of an authentic, rural folk culture or examinations of the complexities of highbrow black life did not represent the boundaries of African American art in the Renaissance. Experimental, genre-busting literature like Jean Toomer's *Cane* sat alongside the militancy of Jamaican poet Claude McKay's "If We Must Die," which in turn shared a stage with the work of blues artists like Ma Rainey and Bessie Smith. Painter Aaron Douglas married African and modernist aesthetics in his work, while sculptor Augusta Savage challenged collectors' and patrons' pursuit of the fetishized native in art.

In this regard, Savage was aligned with critics who were troubled by what scholars now call the "white gaze." The term could refer literally to white audiences at segregated Harlem nightclubs who watched African American performers and participated as onlookers of the social scene or those in Paris, where dancer Josephine Baker mesmerized fans with her notorious and titillating "Banana Dance." Whether in Harlem or Paris or elsewhere, the white gaze also refers to white fascination with black culture. Prominent patrons like the art collector Albert Barnes praised the "authentic and native talent" of a "primitive race." As condescending as Barnes's language sounds, it was meant admiringly: he believed that because blacks were culturally less developed than whites, they were in touch with something mysteriously primal and authentic.

New Negro writer Langston Hughes had a different interpretation of black cultural talent. In his iconic poem, "The Negro Speaks of Rivers," Hughes placed himself (and, by extension, black people across time and space) next to the rivers that cradled civilizations across time: he bathed in the Euphrates, built his home near the

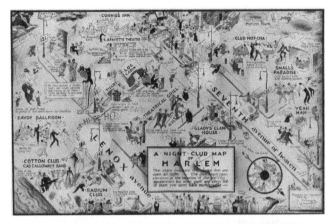

6. African American illustrator E. Simms Campbell published his "Night-Club Map of Harlem" in 1933, capturing the neighborhood's vibrant geography in an image that highlights popular clubs (the Cotton Club, Small's, Connie's Inn), star performers (Cab Calloway, Gladys Bentley, Earl "Snake-Hips" Tucker), and the street-level goings-on of black residents and white spectators alike.

Congo, labored by the Nile, and watched the sun set over the Mississippi. "I've known rivers ancient as the world and older than the flow of human blood in human veins," he wrote.

White Americans declared during Redemption and beyond that African Americans deserved nothing more than second-class status because they were so far removed from the blessings of civilization. Hughes and his fellow New Negro artists and intellectuals felt otherwise and were certain that they were perfectly situated to build a brilliant future on the foundation of a remarkable past. This conviction rings clearly in the closing lines of Hughes's 1926 essay, "The Negro Artist and the Racial Mountain": "We younger Negro artists who create now intend to express our individual dark-skinned selves without fear or shame.... We build our temples for tomorrow, strong as we know how, and we stand on top of the mountain, free within ourselves."

Chapter 5

The making of the modern Civil Rights Movement(s)

In March 1964 performer Nina Simone walked onstage at Carnegie Hall, welcomed by an adoring audience. What the largely white audience could not know was that Simone was about to introduce them to the first of her civil rights songs, "Mississippi Goddam," a stinging lament of the power of an angry, recalcitrant South. Simone's heartbreak was palpable:

> Hound dogs on my trail
> School children sitting in jail
> Black cat cross my path
> I think every day's gonna be my last.

Simone was moved to write these words just months after Martin Luther King Jr. gave his transcendent "I Have a Dream" speech at the March on Washington. What had gone wrong?

Answering that question with the richness it deserves requires more than a cursory exploration of that moment in the country's history. The modern civil rights movement is frequently hailed as an era when the country's better angels tackled the difficult and lingering challenges of systemic segregation and racism. Telling that version of the past means trading in mythology. The history of the modern civil rights movement is far more nuanced than our national narrative allows.

This history of the movement also has roots that extend deep into the early decades of the twentieth century. The 1930s is a good starting point. The giddiness of the Jazz Age collapsed when the stock market crashed in 1929. African Americans were the hardest hit in the ensuing Great Depression. Yet these conditions formed the seedbed for the modern civil rights movement as African Americans articulated new political strategies, gathering momentum amid despair.

For African Americans, Franklin Delano Roosevelt's New Deal—a massive experiment in big government that offered myriad forms of federal intervention and relief—had a varied impact. Many nominally nondiscriminatory New Deal programs were run by local administrators who upheld racist practices, or the programs were structured such that African Americans could not benefit from the assistance they offered. The National Recovery Act (NRA) is an example of the latter. It guaranteed minimum wages for workers in many mechanical and industrial jobs, but not for those in agricultural and domestic jobs—which employed vast numbers of African Americans (this was particularly true for black women when it came to domestic service). This negative disparate impact helps to explain why African Americans called the NRA by other names: Negro Rights Abused, Negro Removal Act, Negroes Ruined Again.

Despite a mixed record with respect to day-to-day life, the New Deal was an overwhelming success in terms of political symbolism. This symbolism, coupled with the New Deal's real interventions, informed a massive shift: over the course of the 1930s, African Americans began to turn their backs on the Republican Party to align with northern Democrats.

While the New Deal at least signaled the hope of forward progress, there were still horrifying setbacks that pointed to the persistence of racism and racist practices. In March 1931 nine African American teenagers traveling on a freight train passing near Scottsboro, Alabama, were arrested and accused of raping two white women who were also on the train—whom the teens would claim they had never seen until the moment of their arrest. Ranging in age from thirteen to twenty, they became known as the Scottsboro Boys. The boys faced an all-white jury and were represented by an incompetent defense attorney. In short order, all but one of the boys was sentenced to death.

The case became a cause célèbre. The NAACP initially held back, hesitant to defend possible rapists. However, the International Labor Defense (ILD), the Communist Party's legal arm, came to the young men's immediate defense. After years of middling success courting African Americans, the Communist Party saw an opportunity and claimed that defending the Scottsboro Boys was tantamount to fighting racism and economic repression. By 1935, the NAACP had adopted a new strategy and partnered with the ILD to form a defense committee dedicated to freeing the defendants. Soon the joint effort secured freedom for half the boys. The rest languished behind bars, one until 1950.

In the midst of this legal travesty, important shifts occurred in the cultural realm. Perhaps most influential was Marian Anderson's Easter Sunday concert in 1939. Anderson, an internationally renowned contralto, was slated to sing in Washington, DC. The deeply conservative Daughters of the American Revolution (DAR), who managed Constitution Hall, the city's largest venue, refused to allow her to perform; she was also barred from singing at the whites-only Central High School. These decisions infuriated African American leaders.

Secretary of the Interior Harold Ickes, once a member of the National Urban League, arranged a concert for Anderson at the Lincoln Memorial. An integrated audience of seventy-five thousand filled the Mall while many more listened to a live radio broadcast. They heard Ickes declare, "Genius, like justice, is blind.... Genius draws no color line." After Ickes's powerful introduction, Anderson walked to the microphone and began her concert with a song familiar to everyone listening, one that also happened to be a powerful rebuke of the DAR: "My country, 'tis of thee, Sweet land of liberty, of thee we sing." The event showed federal officials' willingness to advocate for civil rights, and it symbolically expanded the range of possibilities for African Americans in a segregated nation. Anderson's performance also had global ramifications, given the nation's contemporaneous battle with fascism and Nazism. As the United States became an international power on the cusp of entering World War II, the hypocrisy of a nation that promoted democracy abroad but maintained internal fascistic tendencies became an unavoidable problem. Anderson became a cultural marker of what the United States should be for black citizens and for the world.

African American leaders used this dynamic to their advantage. Consider A. Philip Randolph. In 1917 Randolph cofounded the *Messenger*, a magazine calling for radical black socialist leadership. In 1925 he became head of the Brotherhood of Sleeping Car Porters and Maids, where he advocated for better working conditions and higher wages. Although Randolph's radicalism was often unpopular, this effort earned support from the NAACP, the Urban League, and the American Federation of Labor. Randolph became the country's most significant black labor leader.

In 1940 Randolph and other black leaders met with President Roosevelt to call for the desegregation of the military and for blacks to have access to defense industry jobs. Roosevelt ignored them, wary of losing southern Democrats' political support. In response, Randolph proposed a march on Washington, to take place in July 1941. His plan garnered enormous enthusiasm and an anticipated attendance of one hundred thousand. Just before the proposed march, Roosevelt made a deal with Randolph: he would issue an executive order meeting Randolph's demands if Randolph canceled the march.

7. Framed by the columns of the Lincoln Memorial, Marian Anderson was a regal, elegant presence as she sang to a vast audience on the National Mall on Easter Sunday, 1939. Although she looks strikingly alone in this photograph, she would later recall that when she looked out, "there seemed to be people as far as the eye could see."

8. Gordon Parks's 1942 photograph of Ella Watson, who worked as a cleaner in a federal building in Washington, DC, evokes a panoply of associations. Its title, "American Gothic," alludes to Grant Wood's famous painting of the same name; the broom and mop remind us of Watson's hard work; and the vertical stripes of the American flag look almost like prison bars, raising profound questions about race, labor, and citizenship.

On June 25, 1941, Roosevelt signed Executive Order 8802, which prohibited discrimination in defense industries or government because of race, creed, color, or national origin and stipulated that employers and labor organizations facilitate equitable participation in defense industries. The order also established the Fair Employment Practices Committee (FEPC), a watchdog organization that could encourage companies to follow its directives. Although EO 8802 did not end military segregation, it was clear that presidents could no longer ignore African American leaders.

When Harry Truman became president in 1945, the Democratic Party was on the verge of a split. Southern Democrats, angered by federal support for African Americans, confronted Truman. To placate them, he allowed Congress to kill the FEPC. But Truman, recognizing that he needed African American votes, also created the President's Commission on Civil Rights. In 1947 the commission issued a landmark report, "To Secure These Rights." It called for equal educational opportunities, housing, and jobs. Specific proposals included anti-lynching and anti–poll tax laws, a permanent FEPC, and a stronger Civil Rights Division of the Department of Justice. The commission went further than both southern Democrats and Truman had imagined. In 1948 Truman called for its recommendations to be implemented. Furious southerners threatened a filibuster.

Lacking congressional support, Truman used executive authority. He bolstered the Civil Rights Division, appointed the first black federal judge, and named several African Americans to high-ranking administrative positions. Two of his executive orders, 9980 and 9981, stand out. The former established fair employment practices in the federal government, while the latter abolished segregation in the armed forces and ordered full integration of all services. Truman was making clear and tactical political moves to appeal to the African American vote.

But were they enough? As the 1948 election approached, Truman faced a challenge from progressive Henry Wallace, Roosevelt's former vice president. He also had to deal with conservative southern Democrats, who opposed a strong civil rights platform at the Democratic National Convention. When Truman brought the platform to the floor regardless, conservative Democrats bolted and formed the so-called Dixiecrat Party, with South Carolina governor Strom Thurmond as its candidate. Truman won the presidency by a hair's breadth. African American voters' support made his victory possible.

Alongside political activists like Randolph, African American lawyers were key agents of change in this era. Under Charles Hamilton Houston's leadership in the early 1930s, Howard University Law School became a training ground for civil rights attorneys. Its most famous student was Thurgood Marshall. A Maryland native who had been denied admission to the whites-only University of Maryland School of Law, Marshall found at Howard a boot camp for legal training with special attention to civil rights.

After graduating in 1933, Marshall started his own practice in Baltimore. A year later he became affiliated with the NAACP and scored his first major victory in *Murray v. Pearson* (1935). The case, which had made its way to the Supreme Court, involved a black student, Donald Murray, who was denied entrance to the University of Maryland School of Law. Together with Houston, now head of the NAACP's Legal Defense Fund, Marshall successfully argued that because Maryland did not have a separate and equal facility for blacks, it was obliged to admit Murray. Similar successful cases followed in which schools of law were ordered to open their doors to African American applicants: most notably, *Gaines v. Canada* (University of Missouri School of Law, 1938) and *Sipuel v. Oklahoma* (University of Oklahoma School of Law, 1948). None of these cases challenged *Plessy v. Ferguson* directly; instead, they sought to prove that segregated facilities were deeply unequal, in direct violation of the principle outlined in the Supreme Court's 1896 *Plessy* decision. Marshall and his team were winning cases pertaining to graduate and professional school students, but it became clear that the NAACP's target was secondary and primary schools.

Eventually, five separate cases in South Carolina, Virginia, Kansas, Delaware, and Washington, DC, rose to the Supreme Court. The Court bundled them into *Brown v. Board of Education of Topeka*. In the Court's unanimous May 1954 ruling, Chief Justice Earl Warren wrote, "Separate educational facilities are inherently unequal. Therefore, we hold that the plaintiffs and others similarly situated for whom the actions have been brought are, by reason of the segregation complained of, deprived of the equal protection of the laws guaranteed by the Fourteenth Amendment." The watershed ruling showed unambiguously that "separate but equal" was unconstitutional.

Significantly, *Brown* tasked local school districts with deciding how best to desegregate. Governors in South Carolina, Georgia, and Mississippi threatened to abolish public schools (*Brown* did not apply to private schools). A year after *Brown*, the Court issued what is known as *Brown II*, which declared that desegregation should proceed "with all deliberate speed." It was a damningly vague edict with enduring ramifications. State governments and school boards dragged their feet, declaring that a go-slow approach was the best way to keep the peace.

While *Brown II* may have felt akin to a semantic exercise, there was less ambiguity on the ground in southern cities. Events in Montgomery, Alabama, in late 1955 made as much clear. There, local citizens organized themselves into one of the most determined economic protests in the nation's history. The thirteen-month Montgomery Bus Boycott certainly deserves its place in national lore, but the truth behind the boycott offers an even more compelling portrait of African Americans' demand to be recognized as citizens.

The mythic narrative tells of a tired seamstress named Rosa Parks, who sat in a whites-only section of a city bus, refused to give up her seat, and was arrested. Martin Luther King Jr. came to her rescue and heroically led the ensuing boycott. That history obscures much. Well before Parks refused to move, for example, the Women's Political Council, a Montgomery organization of middle-class black women led by Jo Ann Gibson Robinson, expressed frustration to black ministers and city officials about how African Americans were treated on buses and in stores. The group proposed an economic boycott, hoping to garner community support. Powerful men rejected their ideas, often with gendered condescension. Yet their efforts show that long before the charismatic Dr. King captured the nation's attention, black women organizers were central to the development of the civil rights movement's tactics and strategies.

Parks's actions, moreover, were not spontaneous. While typically portrayed as a respectable person victimized by an unjust system, Parks actually trained at a civil rights institute, Tennessee's Highlander Folk School, before her arrest. At Highlander, Parks met with white radicals, labor organizers, Communists, and African American activists and learned about nonviolent civil disobedience. And while it is important to recognize Parks for her unflinching bravery, she was not the first African American to stand up to segregated practices in Montgomery's public transit system. A few weeks prior to Parks's refusal, a young woman named Claudette Colvin was arrested in a similar situation. Colvin, however, was a pregnant, unmarried teenager, and organizers believed that she was not the right face of the boycott in a conservative southern city. They needed someone who met narrow standards of respectability.

The investment in respectability was a safeguard against the abiding threat of violence. In Mississippi this violence took on gothic proportions. In 1955 several black voting-rights advocates were murdered, one on a courthouse lawn. The president of a local NAACP chapter was shot after refusing to remove his name from the voting register. And then there was the murder of Emmett Till.

Till, a fourteen-year-old boy from Chicago visiting family members, allegedly whistled at a white woman outside a local store. He was abducted and beaten, wrapped in barbed wire, and then tied to farm equipment before being thrown off a bridge. After his body was recovered, his mother, Mamie Till Bradley, insisted upon an open casket at the funeral so that the world could see what had happened to her child. Images of Till's corpse were published in *Jet* magazine, horrifying a generation of black readers. At the trial of the men accused of Till's murder, an all-white jury deliberated for just sixty-seven minutes before finding the defendants not guilty. Soon after, *Look* magazine published an interview with those same defendants, who admitted they had killed Till. It was a spectacular, egregious case of violence gone unpunished, and it demonstrated to all African Americans how precarious their existence was in the Deep South.

The importance that civil rights activists placed on respectability could also be seen in events in Little Rock, Arkansas, in 1957. That year, a small group of outstanding students, eventually known as the Little Rock Nine, were handpicked to integrate Central High School. Resistance was fierce. Governor Orval Faubus called in the Arkansas National Guard to prevent integration. President Eisenhower (who was not a strong proponent of integration but disapproved of the state's flouting of federal law) sent in the 101st Airborne to escort the students into the high school. Once inside, however, the Little Rock Nine endured social taunts and physical abuse. One student had lye thrown in her face and was almost permanently blinded. Despite these threats, the students were expected to ignore the abuse. They had to prove that they were better than the small-minded people who were harassing them. The challenge, however, took a deep personal toll. One of the nine,

Melba Beals, wrote in her diary that her New Year's resolution was to "do my best to stay alive" until the end of the school year.

Central to the mythological version of the civil rights movement is Martin Luther King Jr. King was, in so many ways, exceptional, but even his history demonstrates that the familiar narratives have to be reconsidered. Raised in a family of ministers, King had a raucous adolescence before attending seminary and obtaining a PhD in theology at Boston University. He became the leader of the Dexter Avenue Baptist Church in Montgomery, Alabama, known for its conservative congregation. With his wife, Coretta, and their young child, he planned on a quiet life, but local and national politics would demand otherwise. In Montgomery, the Women's Political Council was agitating for an economic boycott, and black ministers felt pressured to act. After Rosa Parks's arrest, King was thrust into the limelight. Other ministers cajoled him into leading the bus boycott. King, it turned out, was up to the challenge. In a hastily written speech the night before the boycott's launch, King told the overflow crowd that their cause was just: "We are not wrong. If we are wrong, the Supreme Court of this nation is wrong. If we are wrong, the Constitution of the United States is wrong. If we are wrong, God Almighty is wrong. If we are wrong, Jesus of Nazareth was merely a utopian dreamer that never came down to Earth." King's decision to align the rule of law with the Christian ideal of justice elevated the enduring, secular question of who could be a citizen to a level where it could exist above critique or disregard.

In late 1956, the Supreme Court ruled in favor of the activists and forced the bus system to integrate. With the boycott's success, organizers sought to build upon the energy of the moment. They founded the Southern Christian Leadership Conference (SCLC), one of the most important civil rights organizations of the next several decades. King's popularity skyrocketed. In 1960, he left his church to focus entirely on the movement.

The SCLC was built upon King's charisma and success, but tensions always rippled under the organization's surface. King and Bayard Rustin, his chief strategist, disagreed over key facets of the SCLC's structure, including the role of religion in the movement. The SCLC also clashed with established organizations like the NAACP, which saw the new organization and its charismatic leader as competitors for members and funds. Meanwhile, the NAACP faced its own identity crisis, as some members became more militant and called for violence. As these conflicts demonstrate, no single group or person had sole control of the movement.

Exemplifying this wildcat mentality was an event that occurred on February 1, 1960, in Greensboro, North Carolina. Four students from the historically black college North Carolina A&T sat at the whites-only lunch counter at the local Woolworth's drugstore. When the waitress refused to serve them, they stayed in their seats. This was not the first sit-in—labor and civil rights organizers had used the tactic for decades—but amid widespread frustration, this one took off. Sit-ins spread across the South, reaching sixty cities within weeks. Young people, well dressed and impeccably mannered, took up space and silently protested the treatment they received.

Tapping into this energy, SCLC organizer Ella Baker assembled a youth conference in Raleigh, North Carolina, leading to the formation of the Student Nonviolent Coordinating Committee (SNCC). SNCC became a barometer of the movement's ideological evolution throughout the 1960s. At its founding, it was an interracial, nonviolent group composed of college-aged individuals. It initially operated under SCLC's umbrella but soon began to chafe under that organization's top-down leadership structure. (Ella Baker's role in the movement should not be understated. However, until recently, it was. Her work and that of other local activists, many of them also women, had been overlooked in favor of the mythic figures who played outsized roles in the modern civil rights movement narrative.)

One of the earliest tests for SNCC members came in 1961 when they participated in Freedom Rides that had been organized by the Congress of Racial Equality (CORE). These bus rides—with blacks and whites sitting together—were designed to travel from the North into the Deep South to challenge southern segregationist practices that ran afoul of federal law. Angry white resisters attacked activists in several southern bus stations, but the violence escalated dramatically once the first buses crossed into Alabama. In Anniston, mobs threw smoke bombs at the first bus, slashed its tires, set the bus on fire, and beat riders as they tried to escape. Birmingham's commissioner of public safety, Bull Connor, let the riders be attacked by a mob while he delayed sending in police.

It bordered on the predictable that this kind of violence transpired in Birmingham and under Connor's watch. Between 1957 and 1963, the city earned the nickname "Bombingham," with eighteen unsolved bombings in black neighborhoods. By 1962, city leaders privatized Birmingham's parks, playgrounds, pools, and golf courses in an effort to fight the integration of public spaces. Connor was at the center of this resistance.

Martin Luther King Jr. came to the town in 1963 and was soon thrown in jail with fifty other activists for violating a court order against protests. Police placed him in solitary confinement and cut off his access to the outside world, terrifying his family and friends. Birmingham's white moderate clergy, frustrated by the way King antagonized local authorities, published a chastising article that asked him to slow down. King responded with his now-lauded "Letter from Birmingham Jail." He wrote, "We have waited for more than 340 years for our constitutional and God-given rights. . . . Perhaps it is easy for those who have never felt the stinging darts of segregation to say, 'Wait.' [But] there comes a time when the cup of endurance runs over, and men are no longer willing to be plunged into the abyss of despair."

Meanwhile, on the Birmingham streets, Connor responded viciously to a series of marches, terrorizing protesters with police dogs and fire hoses. King and his circle decided to raise the stakes in the conflict by bringing in children to occupy the frontlines, knowing this would attract the media and shock the nation. On May 2, 1963, the first day of the so-called Birmingham Children's Crusade, more than one thousand children left school to march in the streets. Hundreds, ages six through eighteen, were thrown in jail. President John F. Kennedy and his brother, Attorney General Robert F. Kennedy, were horrified. The plan worked insofar as public places began to integrate. But violence remained omnipresent.

In due course, a civil rights bill was introduced. Focused on federal enforcement, it would outlaw segregation in interstate public accommodations, allow the attorney general to initiate school integration suits, and cut off funding to discriminatory federal programs. In support of the bill, groups including SCLC, CORE, NAACP, SNCC, and the Urban League called for a march on Washington. President Kennedy tried to stop civil rights leaders from agitating, but they refused to back down. Eventually, he relented and endorsed the march, albeit on the conditions that officials could preview planned speeches and cut the sound system if necessary.

The March on Washington took place on August 28, 1963. Often remembered as a moment of benevolence and transcendence, the reality was more complex. To start with, its full name was the March on Washington for Jobs and Freedom. It involved labor movements, religious organizations, and civil rights organizations that called for the passage of the civil rights bill as well as a two-dollar minimum wage, immediate school desegregation, a public works program, and action to ban employment discrimination. Behind the scenes, there were heated arguments about the content of some speeches. For instance, SNCC leader John Lewis planned to give a speech calling out the Kennedy administration's moral failings and go-slow approach to justice. Even those who concurred with Lewis's ideas thought they were too antagonistic given the circumstances. With federal agents ready to cut the power to the amplification system, Lewis finally agreed to an edited speech.

Soon after Lewis's speech, King stepped to the microphone. The closing paragraphs of his celebrated speech are part of our national memory: "I have a dream that one day this nation will rise up and live out the true meaning of its creed: 'We hold these truths to be self-evident, that all men are created equal.' . . . I have a dream that my four little children will one day live in a nation where they will not be judged by the color of their skin but by the content of their character." That excerpt, however, is often used misleadingly to imply that King was focused only on imagining a better future. Consider another very different excerpt from earlier in the speech:

> When the architects of our republic wrote the magnificent words of the Constitution and the Declaration of Independence, they were signing a promissory note to which every American was to fall heir. . . . It is obvious today that America has defaulted on this promissory note, insofar as her citizens of color are concerned. Instead of honoring this sacred obligation, America has given the Negro people a bad check, a check which has come back marked "insufficient funds."

Drawing on the terms of capital, King called for the nation to meet its legal and ethical mandates. This was no hopeful reverie.

Keeping these nuances in mind, the march undeniably inspired a transcendent hope. However, that feeling was shattered two weeks later when, on September 15, an explosion outside the 16th Street Baptist Church in Birmingham killed four girls inside. This terrorist attack led Nina Simone to write "Mississippi Goddam." Simone criticized anyone who counseled patience:

Yes, you lied to me all these years
You told me to wash and clean my ears
And talk real fine just like a lady
And you'd stop calling me Sister Sadie
Oh but this whole country is full of lies
You're all gonna die and die like flies
I don't trust you any more
You keep on saying "Go slow!"

To hell with respectability, Simone said. To hell with the beloved country King invoked. Children were being attacked and murdered with impunity. Something had to change.

Asked about the March on Washington, the ever-provocative Nation of Islam spokesman Malcolm X said, "It was a sellout.... They told those negroes what time to hit town, how to come,

9. Nina Simone and James Baldwin, two of the civil rights era's most important voices, share a moment of joy and laughter.

where to stop, what signs to carry, what song to sing, what speech they could make, and what speech they couldn't make; and then told them to get out of town by sundown." Such incendiary rhetoric made Malcolm X famous—or infamous. In speeches like "The Ballot or the Bullet," he declared, "It's the ballot or the bullet. It's liberty or it's death. It's freedom for everybody or freedom for nobody." In "After the Bombing," he argued, "I wouldn't call on anybody to be violent without a cause. But I think the black man in this country, above and beyond people all over the world, will be more justified when he stands up and starts to protect himself, no matter how many necks he has to break or heads he has to crack."

Malcolm X's rhetoric set him apart from other civil rights leaders, but his ideas had ample precedent. He demanded civil rights, as black leaders had since emancipation. His embrace of self-defense and violence if necessary also had precursors. Situating Malcolm X historically is important because he, like King, is often frozen in time, his ideas oversimplified to popularize and commodify his image.

This polarizing activist was born Malcolm Little in 1925; his father was a minister and UNIA organizer. Malcolm dropped out of school at a young age and became a hustler and petty thief. At twenty-one, he was sent to prison for burglary and larceny. In prison, he underwent a religious conversion and became a member of the Lost Found Nation of Islam in the Wilderness of North America, or the Nation of Islam (NOI). He adopted the name Malcolm X in reference to enslaved people who rejected their masters' last names, claiming their own.

Shortly after leaving prison, Malcolm X became an assistant minister at Detroit Temple No. 1, the NOI's headquarters. Cognizant of Malcolm X's skill and charisma, NOI spiritual head Elijah Muhammad appointed him minister of the Harlem temple, then named him a national spokesman. The NOI grew quickly, from several hundred followers in the 1950s to more than ten thousand by the early 1960s. It established new temples, purchased radio stations, and opened stores. As a religious organization, the NOI refused to participate in politics. It projected social conservatism, recalling Booker T. Washington's notions of self-help and self-discipline. It was racially separatist, rejecting the integrationist logic of SNCC and the NAACP.

Soon, the increasingly popular NOI faced internal turmoil. There were rumors about Elijah Muhammad's inappropriate relationships with teenage girls, whisperings about financial improprieties, frustration regarding the NOI's apolitical stance, and simmering tension between Malcolm X and Elijah Muhammad. When Kennedy was assassinated in November 1963, Malcolm X called it "a case of the chickens coming home to roost." He was referring to Kennedy's presidential saber rattling, but the comment horrified the country. Elijah Muhammad reasserted control, silencing Malcolm X for ninety days. During the moratorium, Malcolm X broke from the NOI. He established both a religious organization, the Muslim Mosque Incorporated, and a political one, the Organization of Afro-American Unity (OAAU).

Before establishing the OAAU, Malcolm X took a religious journey to Mecca and underwent a profound change of heart on race relations. He met Muslims who looked white, forcing him to refute simplistic ideas about Islam. His political and ethical outlook, like that of many leaders of the era, became increasingly anticapitalist. Changing his name to El-Hajj Malik El-Shabazz, he rejected views he previously espoused, including black separatism, anti-Semitism, opposition to intermarriage, and patriarchal sexism. He came to recognize women's importance to political struggle and sought alliances with nonblack revolutionary groups.

In February 1965, Malcolm X was assassinated by fringe NOI members. His murder came just as his views were evolving, leaving his legacy difficult to assess. For many, his martyrdom legitimized him. His powerful rhetoric and emotionalism lent themselves well to late-1960s orthodoxies. After his death, his ideas established an organizational logic for groups that barely existed during his lifetime.

Ten months before Malcolm X's assassination, activists in Mississippi launched a massive voter registration and education drive called Freedom Summer. Its goal was clear, if challenging: organizing a political party (the Mississippi Freedom Democratic Party) that would recognize African American voting rights and establish freedom schools to promote literacy. Activists went further, creating community centers at which poor African Americans could receive food and clothing while also developing a political consciousness.

On June 20, 1964, the first wave of recruits arrived in Mississippi for Freedom Summer. The next day, three workers disappeared: two white men, Michael Schwerner of Brooklyn and Andrew Goodman of New York City; and a black Mississippian, James Chaney. In August, their bodies were found in an earthen dam near Philadelphia, Mississippi. They had been beaten brutally before being shot to death and hidden. Twenty-one white men were arrested, including the deputy sheriff, but only six received jail time, of just three to six years.

In July, between the activists' disappearance and the subsequent discovery of their bodies, Lyndon Johnson signed the Civil Rights Act. It ensured full access to places of public accommodation, established a permanent Equal Employment Opportunity Commission, banned discrimination in federally funded programs, and gave the attorney general broad enforcement power. White backlash was immediate. George Wallace, the segregationist Alabama governor, ran for president, garnering strong showings in Wisconsin, Indiana, and Maryland. Across the South, public places were privatized to prevent integration.

While the passage of the Civil Rights Act was a great triumph, activists' work wasn't over. Securing the vote was next. In February, a peaceful SCLC voting rights rally in Alabama turned violent when police attacked activists. During the melee, twenty-six-year-old Jimmie Lee Jackson was shot and killed while attempting to shield his mother from a state trooper.

SCLC and SNCC activists formed a plan to march fifty miles from Selma to Montgomery to protest Jackson's murder and police brutality more generally. On March 7, SNCC chairman John Lewis led six hundred protestors over the Edmund Pettus Bridge. State troopers waited on the other side of the bridge, determined to prevent the march from proceeding. On the governor's orders, the troopers attacked the marchers. Captured on live TV, the debacle prompted nationwide outrage. The failed march became known as "Bloody Sunday."

Thousands flocked to Selma for another march two days later, this time with King present. Despite a federal order banning the march, King led a group across the bridge. Again, law enforcement officers waited on the other side. Instead of provoking a fight, King asked the marchers to kneel and pray, then directed them to return to their churches. SNCC leaders were horrified to discover that King had negotiated the whole performance and that police knew in advance of his plan to have the marchers disperse. From their perspective, King had hijacked the march. Finally, two weeks later, the Selma-to-Montgomery march that has been fixed in our national memory proceeded under federal protection. While the march was a success, fissures between SNCC and SCLC cracked wide open. The younger activists no longer trusted King and his perceived manipulation.

On August 6, 1965, Lyndon Johnson signed the Voting Rights Act (VRA). It prohibited states from imposing obstacles to voting; crucially, it allowed the attorney general to send federal examiners to any election site where voting rights might be curtailed. The

VRA showcased the federal government's ability to intercede in local affairs. The effects were clear almost immediately. Between 1964 and 1969, black voter registration in Alabama jumped from under 20 percent of the population to over 60 percent. In Mississippi, that percentage increased from less than 7 percent to more than 65 percent.

Yet securing voting rights was not the sole purpose of the black freedom struggle, nor did that struggle occur only in the South. Five days after the VRA passed, the Watts community in Los Angeles went up in flames. Watts, where many African Americans settled during World War II, was not wealthy, but it was not as impoverished as the rural South or the Chicago slums. Its residents had rights that southerners had not yet attained. Regardless, African American residents of Watts suffered from a sense of economic malaise and sociopolitical hopelessness. They understood that formal rights did not guarantee equality.

The flashpoint for the uprising was an arrest gone bad. Over several days, thirty-four people died and more than one thousand were injured. Thirty-five thousand people were deemed active rioters. Property damage exceeded $200 million; fires burned while snipers shot at emergency responders. Rioters destroyed stores owned by middle- and upper-class whites, while churches, homes, and libraries were relatively untouched. In this way, the riot was extreme but not mindless; participants decided tactically which institutions to target and which to leave alone.

For white America, the Watts uprising seemed to happen out of the blue. Johnson had signed the Voting Rights Act; wasn't that enough? Clearly, the right to vote and to sit where one wanted on a bus were insufficient. American racism was fundamental and deep. Watts portended a broader shift toward militancy.

By 1965, SNCC was far from SCLC. It became affiliated with the rising New Left and radical student organizations, although relationships with those groups' white leaders could be tense. In the spring of 1966, SNCC leader Stokely Carmichael wrote, "White participation, as practiced in the past, is now obsolete. If we are to proceed toward true liberation, we must cut ourselves off from white people. We must form our own institutions, write our own histories." "The movement," never just one movement and never just about one group or individual, was now splintering in front of everyone's eyes.

Throughout the history of the movement there had always been a commitment to securing full citizenship rights for African Americans, but the approach to that issue changed dramatically from the 1930s to the mid-1960s. African American activists had moved from crafting legal arguments to secure full citizenship toward a moral approach that sought to appeal to the ethics of realizing the country's rhetorical faith in citizenship, only to adopt a militant stance that dared white Americans to deny blacks their birthright.

Chapter 6

The paradoxes of post–civil rights America

In a few short years, the nation watched a civil rights movement catalyze remarkable change throughout the country. The scope and quality of that change, however, were uneven. The nation lurched into foreign conflict, and the beloved nonviolent community of which Martin Luther King Jr. dreamed proved to be more illusory than civil rights activists hoped. Just as the history of the civil rights movement is more complex than the national mythology allows, the terrain of post–civil rights America is similarly unpredictable.

If the civil rights movement was fundamentally about asking the question of what it means to be American, events in the post–civil rights era returned a confusing series of answers that highlighted the potential of an inclusive republic while also reminding Africans Americans of the limited freedoms that others imagined for them. The history of the post–civil rights United States revealed that citizenship for African Americans was no simple construction. Instead, it was a space defined by paradox.

Notably, the Black Power movement confronted mainstream definitions of African American citizenship head on. In October 1966, two students in Oakland, California, Huey Newton and Bobby Seale, embraced Black Power and formed the Black Panther Party for Self-Defense. Newton declared himself minister of defense, and Seale the party's chair. The Panthers' initial platform dealt with issues that had long preoccupied black freedom organizations, while also making a notable departure by connecting African American freedom struggles to global events. Its Marxist ideology cast nationally based struggles in relation to US imperialism in places like Vietnam. It also called for armed self-defense. The Black Panther Party's goals extended beyond getting in the front door of a bus or a restaurant; its ideology encompassed full global citizenship.

Responding to the same frustrations of police brutality that had sparked the Watts riots, the Panthers began to patrol the Oakland police, guns in hand (this was entirely legal at the time). The police were incensed. When the California legislature introduced a bill banning loaded weapons in urban districts, the Panthers traveled to Sacramento in protest, and thirty armed Black Panther Party members entered the capitol building. The resulting media images were vastly different from those that dominated coverage of the southern nonviolent civil rights movement. The Panthers fascinated liberal allies with their charisma, as well as their ability to stump police and other authorities. Their more progressive allies admired the way that the Panthers interlaced local politics with an internationalist agenda.

Although they were mainly known for their provocations, the Panthers were also committed to social service and community organizing. They instituted after-school and literacy activities for black children, established hot-breakfast programs, opened health clinics in medically underserved communities, and organized tests for sickle cell anemia. Much of this work was run by women activists in the group. And perhaps as such, it was work that was overlooked by their contemporaries and, until recently, by historians.

As the Panthers grew, they tapped the charismatic Eldridge Cleaver as minister of information to help with the group's messaging. Cleaver exemplified the members' popular image:

hypermasculine, leather-jacket-wearing, armed, and ready to seize control from the police, or "racist pigs." He was also a convicted rapist and homophobe. In his 1968 book, *Soul on Ice*, Cleaver eviscerated the "so-called molders of public opinion, the writers, politicians, [and] teachers" who "were not equipped to either feel or know that a radical break, a revolutionary leap out of their sight, had taken place in the secret parts of this nation's soul." The critique fascinated left-leaning white Americans, who—enthralled by what they saw as the group's brutal honesty—provided much of the Panthers' funding.

The party's popularity was not without its challenges. In October 1967, Huey Newton was involved in a shootout in which a police officer died. Newton proclaimed his innocence but was arrested. "Free Huey" rallies popped up across the country. Eager to build on this momentum, the Panthers offered SNCC leader Stokely Carmichael the position of prime minister. The Panthers believed that bringing Carmichael on board would quickly lead to a merger of the two organizations. Carmichael, however, failed to consult with other SNCC members, violating a longstanding commitment to group-centered leadership. (Ironically, although the Panthers are historicized as the era's most militant black nationalist group, part of what angered SNCC members was the Panthers' open courting of white support.) The nascent Black Panther Party–SNCC coalition collapsed before it even had a chance to form.

By 1970, Newton was out of prison and back in charge of the Panthers. His efforts to exert singular control were impeded by external forces that were intent on sowing discord. The Federal Bureau of Investigation's antiradical Counter-Intelligence Program (COINTELPRO) had infiltrated the Panthers and fueled paranoia and distrust among its members. Within a few years, the group's heyday ended, and it was essentially defunct.

Despite the failed alliance with the Black Panther Party, SNCC also became caught up in the Black Power passion of the time—and met a similar fate. Following the failed alliance, Carmichael left SNCC and the United States, creating a leadership void. SNCC activist H. Rap Brown stepped into the leadership role and changed the organization's name to the Student *National* Coordinating Committee. In so doing, Brown disavowed nonviolence. Brown's presence at SNCC's helm was short-lived, as he (and SNCC leadership generally) was targeted by COINTELPRO and soon arrested for inciting a riot during a political rally. By 1973, the FBI closed its file on SNCC, which had effectively collapsed.

Even though this was an era of great wealth, social and economic inequalities persisted, and in many cases worsened. A sense of impatience emerged amid an increasingly toxic political environment. The resulting despair was expressed through spasms of violence, particularly in impoverished urban centers. At the same time that the Black Panther Party emerged and SNCC began to radicalize, Martin Luther King Jr. had started to change his political focus and sought to address intransigent problems in the urban North. King had been discussing economics and poverty for years, but now he addressed these issues with vigor. He saw Chicago as a crucible of systemic exploitation: de facto housing segregation, segregated unions, limited educational opportunities, and other inequities propped up by mortgage companies, slum landlords, federal agencies, courts, police, and city administration.

Black Chicagoans initially welcomed King, but it quickly became clear that he was not well suited to their world. In the South, he had focused on discriminatory legal structures and faced a simple political landscape where blacks had no voting presence and a limited activist network. This was not the case in Chicago, where a diverse African American population already had well-established community leaders and organizations, as well as connections to white politicians. Put simply, King stepped on other black activists' toes.

King antagonized others with his increasingly open opposition to the war in Vietnam. A longtime pacifist, he had refrained from criticizing US foreign policy. His fellow movement leaders encouraged King to take this approach, certain that Lyndon Johnson would derail their collective civil rights agenda if any of them spoke out. By the spring of 1967, however, King could not maintain his silence any longer. He began giving detailed lectures about structural inequality, economic super-exploitation, and the immorality of the Cold War. In April King spoke at Manhattan's Riverside Church. From this prominent stage, he declared that Johnson's Great Society had been "shot down on the battlefields of Vietnam." King continued, "I've chosen to preach about the war in Vietnam today because I agree with Dante, that the hottest places in hell are reserved for those who in a period of moral crisis maintain their neutrality." Linking critiques of capitalism and imperialism to the war, he revealed a side of himself the national public did not recognize. Immediately after this speech, Johnson distanced himself from King, determined to silence King's increasingly global and anticapitalist agenda.

Exhausted and dismayed, King continued to link his calls for racial and economic justice. To that end, he began planning a massive protest, the Poor People's Campaign, to call attention to the plight of the multiracial poor. He also lent support to a strike by sanitation workers in Memphis, where the largely black workforce was clamoring for union recognition. At a nighttime rally in Memphis on April 3, 1968, King spoke about his frustrations and fears. "We've got some difficult days ahead," he said. "But it really doesn't matter with me now, because I've been to the mountaintop.... I've seen the Promised Land. I may not get there with you. But I want you to know tonight, that we, as a people, will get to the Promised Land." It was the last speech he would give. The next day, exactly one year after he spoke at Riverside Church against the war in Vietnam, King was assassinated. As the news raced across the country, more than a hundred cities erupted in flames.

Amid confusion and disarray, civil rights leaders sought to honor King's legacy by continuing the Poor People's Campaign. They planned to bring poor people to Washington, DC, for three months, calling for a robust antipoverty package. The first demonstrators arrived in May and set up Resurrection City, a settlement of tents and shacks on the Mall. But the campaign was hobbled by events beyond its control. Thousands more protesters showed up than expected, and the overburdened settlement was plagued by public health problems and safety concerns. Police cleared the settlement six weeks after it opened, the campaign floundering.

In the midst of these assaults on the national political sensibility, African American artists highlighted the paradoxes of increasing poverty in a country of immense wealth and of the abiding problems of second-class citizenship in a country that prided itself on its rhetoric of equality. Nina Simone had pointed to these challenges in songs like "Mississippi Goddam," but the cultural and political analysis in the late 1960s and early 1970s took on a more pointed tone.

For example, in 1971, spoken word artist Gil Scott-Heron critiqued corporate capitalism in "The Revolution Will Not Be Televised" and, a year earlier, excoriated the economic inequalities of American life in "Whitey on the Moon." In the latter piece Scott-Heron contrasted excessive funding of the space race and the government's failure to assist African Americans living in squalor: "A rat done bit my sister Nell, and Whitey's on the moon."

Soul singer Marvin Gaye was on a similar path. Previously known for sweet love songs, he released *What's Going On* in 1971, an album addressing the war in Vietnam, environmental degradation, poverty, and urban decay. In "Inner City Blues," Gaye painted a dystopic picture: "Crime is increasing / Trigger-happy policing / Panic is spreading / God knows where we're heading." In "What's Happening, Brother" a Vietnam vet has returned home and is dismayed about the state of the country. The song powerfully captured the moral confusion of the era:

> War is hell, when will it end,
> When will people start getting together again
> Are things really getting better, like the newspaper said
> What else is new my friend, besides what I read
> Can't find no work, can't find no job my friend
> Money is tighter than it's ever been
> Say man, I just don't understand
> What's going on across this land.

These cultural texts spoke to a profound unrest and anger at the core of American life, which was exacerbated by changing economic and social conditions. To many African Americans, the idea of lost national innocence was nothing new. African American women in particular were acutely disdainful of the country's pronouncements of equality. Denied full citizenship on the basis of "double jeopardy"—being black and being female— they were sidelined in movements for civil rights and women's rights alike. Even vanguard organizations like the Black Panthers were not immune: Elaine Brown, who became leader of the Panthers in the early 1970s, once recalled a meeting when she and other women were forced to wait to eat until the men were served. The largely white feminist movement suffered from similar blind spots. In 1963, Betty Friedan published *The Feminine Mystique*, a bestseller that urged white, middle-class women to get out of the home and into the workplace. For black women, this advice seemed irrelevant; they had always worked outside their own home, often in someone else's as domestics.

African American women were also blamed for societal failures. In 1965, Daniel Patrick Moynihan, the assistant secretary of labor, published "The Negro Family: The Case for National Action" (also known as the Moynihan Report). The report, which would set welfare policy standards for the next generation, charted the economic and social deprivation that emerged from slavery. It concluded that African Americans were caught in a "tangle of pathology" resulting from women-headed households. Moynihan wrote, "The Negro community has been forced into a matriarchal structure which, because it is so out of line with the rest of the American society, seriously retards the progress of the group as a whole." African Americans were outraged. Without denying the reality of poverty in black communities, they were angry that Moynihan depicted them as a problem for white America to solve.

African American women had long issued trenchant critiques of US racism and sexism. But in the 1970s, they articulated a new black feminism that garnered notice. One group, formed partly in response to the Moynihan Report, was the National Welfare Rights Organization (NWRO). Among its founders was Johnnie Tillmon, a black woman and former welfare recipient. Tillmon pursued a practical agenda of decent wages, access to education and job training, medical care for women and children, and daycare; the NWRO also opposed welfare policies that reinforced the patriarchal notion that men should support families. Tillmon and other NWRO activists drew clear connections between welfare rights and civil rights, explaining that welfare was an economic necessity, not the reflection of women's moral failings as the Moynihan Report suggested.

Simultaneous with grassroots efforts like the NWRO, there was a change in the national political landscape. The passage of the Voting Rights Act made an immediate and substantive difference throughout the country. The number of black voters skyrocketed, and African Americans were elected to various positions in parts of the country, like the Southeast, where they had not held office since Reconstruction, if ever. African Americans also began to form a small but critical mass in Congress, and in 1969, they established the Congressional Black Caucus. It aimed to bring together legislators with shared interests and functioned like a political action group.

Tapping into this new opportunity for formal power, a group of political operatives organized the National Black Political Convention in Gary, Indiana, in 1972. This was an attempt to forge a new black political voice, and it included activists and mainstream politicians. The convention's theme was "Unity Without Uniformity," a concept that was tested throughout the gathering as radical activists confronted establishment politicians about their ideas and actions. The convention exposed the diversity of political opinion within black America, but it ended without sending a clear message.

One of the convention's more prominent attendees was Shirley Chisholm of Brooklyn, the first African American woman to represent New York in the House of Representatives. Chisholm had declared her candidacy for president and hoped to gain support at the convention. A coalition politician and member of the predominantly white National Organization for Women (NOW), she found herself abandoned as cold political reality set in. African American politicians and white women saw her campaign as a long shot, so both groups aligned themselves with more likely contenders. It was a crushing blow that affirmed the double-jeopardy status that encumbered black women.

The National Black Feminist Organization (NBFO), established in 1973, had an ideologically broad agenda. Like the NWRO, it addressed practical issues like welfare and unemployment, but it also took up issues typically associated with the white feminist movement, such as abortion rights, and it critiqued white-oriented beauty standards. Perhaps predictably, the group met with a strong backlash. It was accused of hampering *"the"* black movement and of being man-hating, in large part because it welcomed lesbians. Although short-lived, the NBFO exposed hot-button issues and inspired other black feminist groups.

One of the most prominent of these was the Combahee River Collective. In a now-famous statement, the group's members declared, "We see black feminism as the logical political movement to combat the manifold and simultaneous oppression that all women of color face." The statement continued, "If black women were free, it would mean that everyone else would have to be free, since our freedom would necessitate the destruction of all the systems of oppression." Black feminists rejected the narrow focus and racial exclusivity that defined so many white feminist groups, confronting instead multiple interlocking oppressive systems. These changes traveled beyond traditional politics. Black women writers made major contributions to new sensibilities about what a black voice could sound like and who could speak for the race. Toni Morrison (*The Bluest Eye* in 1970), Toni Cade Bambara (*The Black Woman* in 1970), and Alice Walker (*Meridian* in 1976) are but a few of the authors who burst onto the literary scene, remaking it in the process.

Jesse Jackson's rise to prominence reflects the era's shifting politics. A graduate of North Carolina A&T, Jackson was educated in an environment suffused with activism. After college he went on to the Chicago Theological Seminary, then traveled to Selma in the wake of Bloody Sunday, seeing that moment as a call to serve. Among a coterie of talented young activists, Jackson stood out, largely because of his rhetorical skills. Through willpower and charisma, he talked his way into King's inner circle.

The SCLC sent Jackson back to Chicago, where he established Operation Breadbasket, an organization that aimed to diversify business opportunities and services in the city's black community. Relying on economic boycotts and community organizing, Jackson was highly successful. Unlike earlier boycotts, which focused on diversifying the lower-class workforce, Operation Breadbasket emphasized the hiring of black managers. With SCLC's support, Jackson took the project national; his star was rising.

Success burnished Jackson's ego and caused friction with other activists. By 1971, he had split from SCLC and formed the

Chicago-based Operation PUSH (People United to Serve Humanity). Through Operation PUSH, Jackson became a black ambassador to white corporate America, able both to rally black grassroots audiences *and* to massage "the system."

(Jackson parlayed his success on this front into a presidential run in 1984. It was a largely symbolic campaign, scuttled by his loose affiliation with Louis Farrakhan from the NOI and his use of the slur "Hymietown" to refer to New York City. In 1988, Jackson ran again. Distanced from Farrakhan, and more politically polished, he terrified the Democratic establishment when he won the Michigan primary and, for a time, became the frontrunner.)

Following the collapse of Nixon's presidency and Gerald Ford's lukewarm approach to civil rights during his transitional presidency, Jimmy Carter, a little-known former Democratic governor of Georgia, was elected president in 1976. During his presidency, Nixon had used race-based affirmative action cynically as a wedge issue to divide African Americans and labor unions. In contrast, Carter seemed to have a genuine interest in working with African Americans. He garnered 5.2 million black votes (90 percent of those cast) and won the election by only 1.7 million votes. It appeared that African Americans had delivered Carter to the White House, and there was an expectation of something in return.

Carter appointed an unprecedented number of African Americans to the executive branch: 15 ambassadors, 30 federal judges, 50 sub-cabinet officials, 110 members of advisory boards, and 25 White House staff members. Given the longstanding erasure of black presence, especially southern black presence, at the federal level—the South had not elected *any* African Americans to Congress between Reconstruction and 1972, and Georgia and North Carolina would not do so until 1992—this was a major shift. Yet Carter's presidency was largely ineffective. The economy did not improve, he failed spectacularly in his attempt to rescue hostages at the US embassy in Iran, and a disastrous oil crisis swept the United States.

A former governor of California, Ronald Reagan, saw an opportunity to realize his presidential ambitions. A gifted speaker, Reagan ran on a platform of restoring US pride and introducing new economic models. Reagan declared that big government was the problem and that emphasizing states' rights was the solution. Notoriously, he declared his presidential candidacy at the state fair in Philadelphia, Mississippi. His base was thrilled, while civil rights activists were horrified. To advocate for states' rights in the South and to do so in Philadelphia, Mississippi—where Freedom Summer activists Schwerner, Goodman, and Chaney had been murdered—sent an unmistakable message to potential backers: elect Reagan and you will support someone who is committed to keeping African Americans and their political allies in check. Reagan won by a landslide.

With Reagan's 1980 victory, a new era of national politics began: one marked by a backlash against civil rights and a move toward policies that were racially coded without being explicitly race-based. In an allegedly post–civil rights moment, it was no longer fashionable to race-bait explicitly. However, Reagan, the "Great Communicator," was an expert at talking about racial politics without talking about race, and virtually every politician since has mastered this skill.

This trend was fully realized in the 1988 presidential campaign, featuring George H. W. Bush and Massachusetts Democrat Michael Dukakis. Bush, Reagan's vice president, moved rightward to appease the conservative arm of the Republican Party. His campaign argued that Dukakis was "soft on crime." The phrase seized upon age-old rhetoric linking black men to crime. The Bush campaign found an ideal example in Willie Horton. An African American violent criminal in Massachusetts, Horton mistakenly received a forty-eight-hour furlough via a state rehabilitation program. He failed to return, then attacked a couple and raped a woman. The Bush campaign's ad showed Horton's mug shot, and a voice intoned: "Bush and Dukakis on crime. Bush supports the death penalty for first-degree murderers. Dukakis not only opposes the death penalty, he allowed first-degree murderers to have weekend passes from prison." One of the more notorious ads in modern political campaigning, it reaffirmed the notion that black men were to be feared and that they would benefit if Dukakis were elected. Although Bush quickly denounced the ad, it was aired over and over on the news, amplifying the linkage of race and crime in the public imagination. Bush won the election.

In March 1991 in Los Angeles, a black man named Rodney King got behind the wheel of his car while under the influence. A high-speed chase ensued. A gang of police officers arrested and beat King, who suffered a fractured skull and internal injuries. The beating was captured on video, and subsequently four police officers were charged with assault.

Thirteen months later the officers charged in the Rodney King case were acquitted of using excessive force in King's beating. Riots broke out within hours. Sixty-three people died in the ensuing violence and twelve thousand were arrested; white- and Asian-owned businesses were attacked, resulting in more than $1 billion of property damage. The media sensationalized the events further. For example, footage circulated of a white truck driver, Reginald Denny, who was gruesomely attacked by black men during the riots. Media accounts left out the fact that a group of African Americans saved Denny, and ignored his own protest against being depicted this way. Instead, the narrative simply reiterated the notion that African Americans were violent, rioting criminals.

The language of predation registered at all levels of society. When Thurgood Marshall retired in 1991, President Bush nominated Clarence Thomas to the Supreme Court. Thomas had morphed from a black nationalist and Malcolm X supporter in college into an anti–affirmative action, antiwelfare, and antiabortion activist. Although Bush declared him the most "qualified" nominee he could find, Thomas had barely served on the bench. The NAACP, National Urban League, and National Bar Association all opposed his nomination, while the American Bar Association refused to consider him "well qualified." Regardless, a smooth nomination process ensued—that is, until Anita Hill, who had worked for Thomas, alleged that he had sexually harassed her. She said that Thomas behaved inappropriately in the workplace, where he boasted about his "sexual prowess" and spoke openly about "women having sex with animals and films showing group sex or rape scenes."

Thomas denied the allegations, then infamously declared the situation "nothing but a high-tech lynching for uppity blacks who deign to think for themselves." It was a cynical but politically brilliant move. Although Thomas had previously emphasized his

10. As she testified before the all-male, all-white Senate Judiciary Committee at the Supreme Court confirmation hearing for Clarence Thomas in 1991, Anita Hill maintained a quiet dignity while answering graphic, often hostile questions about sexual harassment.

ostensible commitment to colorblind politics, he now used racialized language to end the inquiry. He was confirmed 52 to 48. The incident was a bellwether for racial politics, and perhaps even more important, it changed conversations about gender discrimination and workplace sexual harassment. Sexual harassment claims doubled in the wake of the imbroglio. The number of women who ran for office increased dramatically as well. *Time* magazine declared 1992 "The Year of the Woman."

Bill Clinton was elected in 1992 following twelve years of Republican control of the White House. African Americans embraced Clinton's promise to form a diverse administration that "looked like America." Problems arose, however, when Clinton nominated black law professor Lani Guinier to be assistant secretary of civil rights. In law review articles, Guinier had advocated "cumulative voting," a process that is designed to secure proportional representation rather than limiting voters to a "winner-takes-all" approach and that actually had been sanctioned repeatedly by the Reagan and Bush Justice Departments. But the conservative media went into attack mode, decrying Guinier as a "quota queen." This phrase evoked the "welfare queen," a 1980s catchphrase used to depict African American women (although most welfare recipients are not black) as blights on the American economy. The word "quota" referred to legal battles over affirmative action. In 1978, the Supreme Court had ruled in *Bakke v. the Regents of the University of California* that admissions quotas were unconstitutional. (The case concerned a white man, Allan Bakke, who had been rejected from medical school at the University of California, Davis, which admitted black and Latinx applicants with lower MCAT scores using a race-based quota system.) Within months Clinton withdrew Guinier's nomination. To liberals, Clinton's decisions suggested a general move away from the commitment to civil rights ideologies.

Meanwhile, court cases took up questions of race, affirmative action, and politics. A series of legal decisions built upon one another, yielding the cumulative effect of narrowing the grounds upon which race could be used as a factor to increase voting opportunities (*Shaw v. Reno*, 1993), to improve competitive opportunities for minority-owned businesses (*Adarand v. Peña*, 1995), or to earn admission to colleges and universities (*Hopwood v. Texas*, 1996).

The most public and contentious of these decisions revolved around university admissions policies. These debates began in earnest with the *Bakke* decision in 1978, continued through cases like *Hopwood*, and then evolved into a new phase in 1997, when Barbara Grutter, a white woman, was rejected by the University of Michigan Law School, which freely admitted that it used race as a "compelling interest" in admissions. Ultimately, the Supreme Court's answer was mixed: student body diversity was a compelling interest, and race could be a factor if used in a narrowly tailored way. Justice Sandra Day O'Connor also noted her belief that within twenty-five years, affirmative action would no longer be necessary.

The courts did not have to wait that long for similar cases to emerge that questioned affirmative action. In 2008, Abigail Fisher, a white woman, sued the University of Texas over its admissions policies, claiming that she was discriminated against on the basis of race. Texas's admissions plan, Fisher argued, violated the equal protection clause of the Fourteenth Amendment. Although Fisher lost her legal fight (and subsequent appeals), her legal team's strategy illustrated one of the important turns in civil rights jurisprudence. Beginning in earnest in the 1990s, civil rights case law was being used by white plaintiffs in an effort to roll back the movement's more controversial gains.

This legal strategy reflected the opinion that the victories of the civil rights movement had gone too far. Even though the movement was committed to finding ways to ensure that the ideals of the Constitution would be realized in everyday life, many conservatives decried the notion that African Americans had been denied full access to equality of opportunity in the period since the Civil War. This was a major faultline in the debates about the meaning of citizenship and the role of race after the civil rights movement. What would it take, given this conservative mindset, for African Americans and their allies to realize that their endless grievances were the true impediment to their progress?

This question began to be tested in unexpected ways when Barack Obama, the recently elected junior US senator from Illinois, decided to run for the presidency in 2007. When Obama, originally considered a relative long shot, started winning one primary after another and became the Democratic frontrunner, the question took on great importance. Obama did not dwell on race-related injuries or insults. He was not naive to the fact, however, that his race mattered to voters in both affirming and damning ways.

By March 2008, Obama had won nine primaries in a row. No other African American had had such success in a presidential campaign. Then, news outlets began to cover the controversial views of Obama's onetime pastor, Reverend Jeremiah Wright of Chicago's Trinity Church. For a year, Obama had been quietly distancing himself from Wright as the latter's critical views about the country's racial hypocrisy began to circulate broadly. When the controversy threatened to overwhelm his campaign, Obama gave a speech at the National Constitution Center in Philadelphia. In that speech, titled "A More Perfect Union," Obama repudiated some of Wright's views, but he did not apologize. Instead, he focused his attention on the scar of race that ran through American history. He acknowledged the need for a more honest dialogue about race and asserted that race was used as a veil to mask other issues. Obama claimed that although Wright's views might sound repugnant, they made sense to many African

11. Speaking in front of the Edmund Pettus Bridge at an event commemorating the fiftieth anniversary of Bloody Sunday and the Selma-to-Montgomery marches, President Barack Obama honored the protesters who had marched there before: "What could be more American," he asked, "than what happened in this place?"

Americans. The nuanced speech was far removed from typical American political discourse on race—which ignored complicated realities and engaged in simple coding of people and behaviors.

When Obama was elected that fall, he embodied the possibilities of a country that in many African Americans' eyes had finally lived up to the ideals written in its founding documents. Obama's election appeared to put to rest the painful paradoxes of the post–civil rights era and the long legacy of racial slavery and social degradation.

This was a new day for a country. Or was it?

In 2009, shortly after the Obama presidency began, the *New York Post* published a cartoon depicting two police officers who had shot a chimpanzee. One officer is depicted saying to the other,

"We'll have to find someone else to write that next stimulus bill." The cartoon clearly evoked the long history of racist connections between African Americans and apes, as well as that of police shooting unarmed black citizens. That same year, the mayor of Los Alamitos, California, sent out emails claiming the need for a watermelon patch on the White House lawn now that Obama was in office.

Epilogue: Stony the road we trod

This book opened with the question *What does it mean to be American?* Although at first glance it is a simple query, upon closer scrutiny one discovers that it is multifaceted. Being American is, in part, an act of declaration, rooted in the principles that guided the establishment of this country and that have been rearticulated at different moments in its history: a faith in the idea of freedom and a pledge to respect liberty and justice for all. Relatedly, being American means, for many, membership in a community of citizens who believe in the rights of assembly, speech, and unfettered access to the ballot box. With an unsettling consistency, however, being American has also been defined in a negative way: not being black.

The history of Africans in colonial America and then African Americans in the United States is filled with troubling examples of the great distance that has separated black individuals from their rightful acceptance as fully human, proper citizens, or as civilized. This distance has been invoked, among other things, to rationalize slavery, to preserve economic and political inequality, to justify sexual assault and mob violence, to deny access to decent education, housing, and employment opportunities, and to stifle dissent. James Baldwin powerfully captured the tension and heartbreak that are at the core of the African American experience: "It comes as a great shock, around the age of five, or six, or seven, to discover that the flag to which you have pledged allegiance, along with everybody else, has not pledged allegiance to you."

But what are we to make of Baldwin's observation? In a country that has seemed so committed to systems of racial degradation, is it ever possible to find redemption or perhaps temporary reprieve in exceptional moments in our nation's past? If so, can we draw lessons from those moments that might inform how we use this history in order to make a better future?

For many Americans, one such exceptional moment was Barack Obama's election. Surely, with the election of the first African American president, the country's citizens had demonstrated that they had emerged from their extended and insolent adolescence. For a time, at least on the day of Obama's first inauguration, it seemed that absolution was at hand. The inauguration itself, though, was a prismatic reminder that being American could be refracted in ways that showed the country in different lights.

Such differences became plain when the Reverend Joseph Lowery, a civil rights pioneer and former head of the Southern Christian Leadership Conference, slowly walked to the microphone on the steps of the nation's capitol and opened his benediction with the following lines:

> God of our weary years,
> God of our silent tears,
> Thou who has brought us thus far along the way;
> Thou who has by thy might,
> Led us into the light,
> Keep us forever in the path, we pray.

These words, offered without comment or contextualization, were heard in different ways by the consuming public. Those who were not African American saw a frail man open a benediction with language that spoke of struggle, humility, faith, and belonging—all fitting qualities for the inauguration of the first black president. The great majority of African Americans, however, knew within moments that Lowery was quoting the final stanza of the song "Lift Ev'ry Voice and Sing." Written in 1900 by James Weldon Johnson and set to music by his brother J. Rosamond five years later, "Lift Ev'ry Voice and Sing" is colloquially known as the black national anthem. In the African American community it is a staple of church services, graduation ceremonies, celebrations, and memorials. Its words serve as a reminder of the difficult path, referred to as the "stony road" in the song's lyrics, that African Americans have traveled, and they speak to the debt that those in the present owe to the hard work and aspirations of their ancestors.

This path, the African American experience, has been challenging to navigate, but it has not been without moments of accomplishment, and sometimes even redemption. On this path is a light—sometimes seemingly close and easily discerned, other times frustratingly distant and obscure—that marks the end of a long journey where one is recognized as a full citizen, unencumbered by racial discrimination, violence, and suspicion. But even during Obama's presidency, when it might have seemed that African Americans were closer to this light than ever before, there were reminders of how treacherous that journey could be. Just a short overview of events from the past decade illuminates the tremendous complexity that defines the African American past and present.

On February 26, 2012, seventeen-year-old Trayvon Martin was walking from a local convenience store to his father's fiancée's house in Sanford, Florida, when he was confronted by George Zimmerman, a local resident. Zimmerman, a volunteer member of the Neighborhood Watch, had already called the police, claiming that Martin looked "suspicious." Before the authorities could arrive, Zimmerman confronted Martin and shot him in the chest, killing him. Zimmerman claimed that Martin attacked him and that he was acting in self-defense. (Florida's Stand Your Ground law allowed citizens to protect themselves with lethal force when being attacked.) Zimmerman was eventually arrested and tried. The jury acquitted him of second-degree murder and manslaughter. Martin's supporters declared that his only "crime" was being a black teenager wearing a hoodie, minding his own business while carrying a bag of candy and a bottle of iced tea.

In the wake of Martin's murder, a grassroots campaign emerged that would become known as Black Lives Matter (BLM). This movement originated with a hashtag, #BlackLivesMatter, by Alicia Garza, Patrisse Cullors, and Opal Tometi. Having no single leader and largely conducted through social media, the BLM movement declared that African Americans had rights, too, and deserved to be treated as citizens in their own country. BLM's assertive tactics tested the patience of police forces (which were accused of wanton violence against African Americans), municipalities (which were accused of perpetuating systems of racial dominance), and entrenched black political leaders (who were accused of being part of the machinery of oppression). Sadly, BLM activists across the country would encounter many more instances in the following years that confirmed for them the contingent nature of black life in modern America.

One of the most infamous moments occurred in Ferguson, Missouri, on August 9, 2014, when eighteen-year-old Michael Brown got into an argument with police officer Darren Wilson. Eyewitness accounts differed radically about what happened next—did Brown run away from Wilson after trying to grab his gun?, were Brown's hands up?, did he charge the officer?—but what is beyond dispute is that Wilson shot Brown six times. Brown's body then lay on the street for four hours while police secured the crime scene, waiting for medical examiners to arrive. Local residents, many deeply frustrated by what they deemed abiding mistreatment at the hands of the local police force, interpreted the long delay before removal of the body as yet another demonstration of disregard for African Americans, even in death. This perceived mistreatment was confirmation for many that black lives, in fact, did not matter to the state. In the wake of Brown's death, protests flared in Ferguson for a week as activists carried signs that said, "Hands Up, Don't Shoot," an expression of their profound distrust of the police and their lament over the perceived worthlessness of black life.

On June 17, 2015, less than one year after Michael Brown's death, Dylann Roof walked into Emanuel African Methodist Episcopal Church in Charleston, South Carolina, ostensibly to join a prayer group. Soon after he sat down he pulled out a gun and opened fire on the parishioners, all African American, murdering nine and injuring a tenth. At first, many southern white politicians claimed that Roof's crime was an act of anti-Christian violence. African Americans, however, saw it as something quite different. The politicians' insistence crumbled when, several days after Roof's capture, investigators found online evidence connecting Roof to a white supremacist manifesto and pictures of him posing with paraphernalia that championed segregation and apartheid. Roof later confessed that he had been radicalized by the postmortem outpouring of support for Trayvon Martin and that he wanted to start a race war in order to secure a just peace for white Americans.

In one of Roof's photographs, he is seen holding a handgun and carrying a small version of the Confederate battle flag. It was a much larger version of the same flag that activist Bree Newsome took down ten days after Roof's rampage. On June 27, Newsome climbed a thirty-foot flagpole at the Confederate War Memorial on the South Carolina State House grounds and came down with the flag in her hands. She and a colleague were immediately arrested by police, and the flag was raised within forty-five minutes. (Still reeling from Roof's white supremacist assault,

South Carolina legislators would soon vote to remove the flag permanently.) In that moment, however, Newsome called attention to this country's deep cultural and political divide between the races. Many whites said that the flag was a symbol of heritage and argued that it deserved to fly in honor of those who respected southern traditions. African Americans viewed the flag through a different lens, seeing it as a symbol of hate and an emblem of a socioeconomic system fueled by racial exploitation and violence.

Newsome's act of protest took place in the early days of a cultural and political moment in which citizens, black and white, began to ask new and critical questions about the memorialization of the Confederacy. In the wake of the Charleston murders, the increasing vitriol from white nationalist groups, and the steadily improving effectiveness of BLM activists, local jurisdictions quickly began to reconsider their support for Confederate memorials.

The town of Charlottesville, Virginia, was no more or less remarkable when it came to these issues. There, city officials had been embroiled for years in back-and-forth debates about removing statues of Confederate generals Robert E. Lee and Stonewall Jackson. Over the course of several months in the spring and summer of 2017, different white nationalist groups marched in Charlottesville to protest the city council's vote to remove the Lee statue. Neo-Nazis and the KKK marched on May 13 and July 8, respectively. On August 11 and 12, several groups, bound by a violent white pride, gathered for a Unite the Right rally. They carried weapons, Confederate battle flags, and Nazi flags while chanting racist and anti-Semitic slogans. Counterprotesters arrived as well, determined to demonstrate their refusal to accede to white supremacist logics. Police did their best to keep the two groups separated. James Fields Jr., a Unite the Right participant, foiled those efforts when he intentionally drove his car into a crowd of counterprotesters, injuring nineteen people and killing activist Heather Heyer.

The nation was reeling when Donald Trump, elected president in 2016 on a platform of overturning Barack Obama's policies, tried to restore calm in Charlottesville. In a rhetorical move that shocked many, Trump decried the "egregious display of hatred, bigotry, and violence—on many sides." Battered by intense political pressure to speak with greater force against the white supremacists and neo-Nazis who organized the rally, Trump clarified his August 12 comment, stating that he condemned the hate groups. On August 15, however, Trump returned to his previous position, stating that there were "fine people on both sides."

Trump ran for office on the slogan "Make America Great Again," a barely implicit suggestion that the country had lost its way during the Obama administration. Trump's political speeches became lightning rods for the disaffected who felt that they had been steadily losing ground in a country that was increasingly diverse and multinational. After eight years of Obama's language of racial reconciliation, Trump repeatedly sent shockwaves through the liberal establishment with statements that seemed to encourage violence toward marginalized people.

And yet even with rising tides of racial violence and a superheated rhetoric from political conservatives that inspired those committed to African American subjugation to continue their work, there were instances of sublime triumph related to what one might refer to as a project of historical repair in the black community. Two such moments were the September 2016 opening of the Smithsonian's National Museum of African American History and Culture (NMAAHC) and the April 2018 opening of the National Memorial for Peace and Justice.

Since 1915, advocates had been calling for a national museum addressing the African American experience. Supporters had come close to securing federal funding in the late 1980s and early 1990s, and final authorization came in 2003. Built adjacent to the

Washington Monument, the NMAAHC became a sensation from the moment its doors opened. Anticipating large crowds, the Smithsonian instituted a timed-entry ticket system. Lonnie Bunch III, the founding director of the museum, felt that this crowd management system would be needed for no more than the first six months of the museum's life. At the time of this writing, three years after the museum opened, the demand remains so high that the museum still relies on timed access. One reason for this unyielding demand is that the museum has become a site of pilgrimage for African American visitors, many of whom never imagined that their story would become part of a public and national narrative.

However astonishing the NMAAHC is, a more striking accomplishment may be the National Memorial for Peace and Justice. This memorial is the brainchild of attorney Bryan Stevenson, founder of the Equal Justice Initiative, a nonprofit organization dedicated to providing legal representation to the indigent and those who have been wrongly accused of crimes. The site, informally known as the National Lynching Memorial, features eight hundred rust-colored, coffin-like, steel rectangles suspended overhead—the weight of so much history hanging in the air. Each rectangle/coffin represents a county where a documented lynching occurred. The names of the nation's more than four thousand lynching victims are engraved on the steel objects, each name linked to the county in which the individual was murdered. This kind of acknowledgment would have been unimaginable a generation ago. Furthermore, the fact that this memorial is in Montgomery, Alabama, near the site of a former slave market, demonstrates a kind of social and intellectual maturity suggesting that some parts of the nation may, in fact, be ready to acknowledge the more nuanced and difficult elements of this country's history.

Even in light of a difficult racial climate, recurring acts of racial violence, and the increasing openness of white supremacist rhetoric, the mere existence of the NMAAHC and the National Memorial for Peace and Justice invites us to consider African American resilience and the investment that black people have made throughout their history in the hope that tomorrow will be better. The opening stanza of "Lift Ev'ry Voice and Sing" speaks to this perseverance and acknowledges that knowing the African American past is the first step toward learning what we have been as a nation of people and, better yet, what we might become:

Lift every voice and sing
Till earth and heaven ring
Ring with the harmonies of Liberty;
Let our rejoicing rise,
High as the list'ning skies,
Let it resound loud as the rolling sea.
Sing a song full of faith that the dark past has taught us,
Sing a song full of the hope that the present has brought us;
Facing the rising sun of our new day begun,
Let us march on till victory is won.

References

Introduction: What does it mean to be American?

"Transcript of the Baldwin versus Buckley Debate at the Cambridge Union," in Nicholas Buccola, *The Fire Is upon Us: James Baldwin, William F. Buckley Jr., and the Debate over Race in America* (Princeton, NJ: Princeton University Press, 2019), 381, 383.

Anna Julia Cooper, *A Voice from the South* (Xenia, OH: Aldine Printing House, 1892), 120–21.

W. E. B. Du Bois, *The Souls of Black Folk* (Chicago: A. C. McClurg, 1903), 3.

Chapter 1: Race, slavery, and ideology in colonial North America

Álvar Núñez Cabeza de Vaca, *The Narrative of Cabeza de Vaca*, trans. and ed. Rolena Adorno and Patrick Charles Pautz (Lincoln: University of Nebraska Press, 2003).

Heather Williams, *American Slavery: A Very Short Introduction* (New York: Oxford University Press, 2014), 4.

See Stephanie Smallwood, *Saltwater Slavery: A Middle Passage from Africa to American Diaspora* (Cambridge, MA: Harvard University Press, 2007); Eric Taylor, *If We Must Die: Shipboard Insurrections in the Era of the Atlantic Slave Trade* (Baton Rouge: Louisiana State University Press, 2009); and Marcus Rediker, *The Slave Ship: A Human History* (New York: Penguin Books, 2014).

Alexander Falconbridge, *An Account of the Slave Trade on the Coast of Africa* (London: J. Phillips, 1788), 25.

Olaudah Equiano, *The Interesting Narrative of the Life of Olaudah Equiano, or Gustavus Vassa, the African. Written by Himself* (London: Printed by the author, 1789), 78–79.

David Eltis, "Construction of the Trans-Atlantic Slave Trade Database: Sources and Methods," Voyages: The Trans-Atlantic Slave Trade Database, 2010, https://slavevoyages.org.

John Hope Franklin and Evelyn Brooks Higginbotham, *From Slavery to Freedom: A History of African Americans*, 9th ed. (New York: McGraw-Hill, 2011), 44.

Bob Janiskee, "Sullivan's Island Was the African-American Ellis Island," *National Parks Traveler*, March 4, 2009, https://www.nationalparkstraveler.org/2009/03/sullivan-s-island-african-american-ellis-island.

See, in general, Walter Johnson, *Soul by Soul: Life Inside the Antebellum Slave Market* (Cambridge, MA: Harvard University Press, 2001).

See Thelma Jennings, "'Us Colored Women Had to Go through a Plenty': Sexual Exploitation of African-American Slave Women," *Journal of Women's History* 1, no. 3 (1999): 45–74.

Edmund Morgan, *American Slavery, American Freedom: The Ordeal of Colonial Virginia* (New York: W. W. Norton), 1975.

See Vincent Carretta, *Phillis Wheatley: Biography of a Genius in Bondage* (Athens: University of Georgia Press, 2011).

Annette Gordon-Reed, *The Hemingses of Monticello: An American Family* (New York: W. W. Norton, 2009).

Thomas Jefferson, *Notes on the State of Virginia* (Paris, 1785), 229.

Chapter 2: Resistance and African American identity before the Civil War

Philip Foner, ed., *The Life and Writings of Frederick Douglass*, vol. 2, *Pre–Civil War Decade, 1850–1860* (New York: International, 1950), 189.

See Saidiya Hartman, *Scenes of Subjection: Terror, Slavery, and Self-Making in Nineteenth-Century America* (New York: Oxford University Press, 1997); and Stephanie Camp, *Closer to Freedom: Enslaved Women and Everyday Resistance in the Plantation South* (Chapel Hill: University of North Carolina, 2004).

See Elizabeth Maddock Dillon and Michael Drexler, eds., *The Haitian Revolution and the Early United States: Histories, Textualities, Geographies* (Philadelphia: University of Pennsylvania Press, 2016).

See David Robertson, *Denmark Vesey: The Buried Story of America's Largest Slave Rebellion and the Man Who Led It* (New York: Knopf, 1999).

David Walker, *Walker's Appeal in Four Articles; Together with a Preamble, to the Coloured Citizens of the World, but in Particular, and Very Expressly, to Those of the United States of America* (Boston: Published by the author, 1829), 73.

Maria Stewart, "Why Sit Ye Here and Die?," in *Maria W. Stewart, America's First Black Woman Political Writer: Essays and Speeches*, ed. Marilyn Richardson (Bloomington: Indiana University Press, 1987), 48.

Harriet Jacobs, *Incidents in the Life of a Slave Girl* (Boston: Published for the author, 1861).

See Nell Irvin Painter, *Sojourner Truth: A Life, A Symbol* (New York: Norton, 1997).

Martin Delany, *The Condition, Elevation, Emigration, and Destiny of the Colored People in the United States, Politically Considered* (Philadelphia: Published by the author, 1852), 155.

Dred Scott v. Sandford, 60 U.S. at 405 (1857).

Toni Morrison, *Beloved* (New York: Knopf, 1987).

Chapter 3: War, freedom, and a nation reconsidered

James McPherson, *Ordeal by Fire: The Civil War and Reconstruction* (New York: Knopf, 1982), 94, 114, 294.

John Brown, "Address to the Court," in *Testimonies of Capt. John Brown, at Harper's Ferry, with his Address to the Court* (New York: American Anti-Slavery Society, 1860), 15.

See Eric Foner, *The Fiery Trial: Abraham Lincoln and American Slavery* (New York: W. W. Norton, 2010).

On the enduring significance of the Fifty-Fourth, see Martin H. Blatt, Thomas J. Brown, and Donald Yacovone, eds., *Hope and Glory: Essays on the Legacy of the 54th Massachusetts Regiment* (Amherst: University of Massachusetts Press, 2001).

Jim Downs, *Sick from Freedom: African-American Illness and Suffering during the Civil War and Reconstruction* (New York: Oxford University Press, 2012), 4.

See Iver Bernstein, *The New York City Draft Riots: Their Significance for American Society and Politics in the Age of the Civil War* (New York: Oxford University Press, 1991), 27–30.

See W. E. B. Du Bois, *Black Reconstruction in America: An Essay toward a History of the Part Which Black Folk Played in the Attempt to Reconstruct Democracy in America, 1860–1880* (New York: Harcourt, Brace, and Company, 1935); and Eric Foner, *Reconstruction: America's Unfinished Revolution, 1863–1877* (New York: Harper and Row, 1988).

See Paul Cimbala and Randall Miller, eds., *The Freedmen's Bureau and Reconstruction: Reconsiderations* (New York: Fordham University Press, 1999).

Chapter 4: Civilization, race, and the politics of uplift

Billie Holiday, vocalist, "Strange Fruit," lyrics by Abel Meeropol, recorded April 20, 1939, Commodore Records C-526.

See Crystal Feimster, *Southern Horrors: Women and the Politics of Rape and Lynching* (Cambridge, MA: Harvard University Press, 2009).

James Allen, Hilton Als, John Lewis, and Leon F. Litwack, *Without Sanctuary: Lynching Photography in America* (Santa Fe, NM: Twin Palms Publishers, 2000).

W. E. B. Du Bois, *Dusk of Dawn: An Essay toward an Autobiography of a Race Concept* (New York: Schocken Books, 1940), 67.

Gail Bederman, *Manliness and Civilization: A Cultural History of Gender and Race in the United States, 1880–1917* (Chicago: University of Chicago Press, 2005), 45–76.

Mia Bay, *To Tell the Truth Freely: The Life of Ida B. Wells* (New York: Hill and Wang, 2009).

See Kevin Gaines, *Uplifting the Race: Black Leadership, Politics, and Culture in the Twentieth Century* (Chapel Hill: University of North Carolina Press, 1996).

Anna Julia Cooper, *A Voice from the South* (Xenia, OH: Aldine Printing House, 1892), 31.

Booker T. Washington, "The Standard Printed Version of the Atlanta Exposition Address," September 18, 1895, in *The Booker T. Washington Papers*, ed. Louis R. Harlan, vol. 3, *1889–95* (Urbana: University of Illinois Press, 1974), 585.

Plessy v. Ferguson 163 US at 551 (1896).

Plessy v. Ferguson 163 US at 562 (1896).

See Cooper, *Voice from the South*.

W. E. B. Du Bois, *The Souls of Black Folk* (Chicago: A. C. McClurg, 1903), 49, 53–54.

See James Grossman, *Land of Hope: Chicago, Black Southerners, and the Great Migration* (Chicago: University of Chicago Press, 1989); and Isabel Wilkerson, *The Warmth of Other Suns: The Epic Story of America's Great Migration* (New York: Random House, 2010).

Rolfe Cobleigh, "Fighting a Vicious Film: Protest against 'The Birth of a Nation,'" Boston Branch of the NAACP, 1915.

W. E. B. Du Bois, "Close Ranks," *Crisis*, July 1918, 111.

Alessandra Lorini, *Rituals of Race: American Public Culture and the Search for Racial Democracy* (Charlottesville: University of Virginia Press, 1999), 245.

Du Bois, "Returning Soldiers," *Crisis*, May 1919, 13.

Marcus Garvey, "Declaration of the Rights of the Negro Peoples of the World," quoted in *Let Nobody Turn Us Around: Voices of Resistance, Reform, and Renewal—An African American Anthology*, ed. Manning Marable and Leith Mullings (Lanham, MD: Rowman and Littlefield, 2003), 259.

Marcus Garvey Jr., "Garveyism: Some Reflections on Its Significance for Today," in *Marcus Garvey and the Vision of Africa*, ed. John Henrik Clarke with Amy Jacques Garvey (New York: Vintage, 1974), 377.

See Marable and Mullings, eds., *Let Nobody Turn Us Around*, 259–73; and Colin Grant, *Negro with a Hat: The Rise and Fall of Marcus Garvey* (New York: Oxford University Press, 2010).

Alain Locke, ed., *The New Negro: An Interpretation* (New York: A. and C. Boni, 1925), 3.

Sterling Brown, *Southern Road* (New York: Harcourt, Brace, and Company, 1932); Zora Neale Hurston, *Mules and Men* (Philadelphia: J. B. Lippincott, 1935); Hurston, *Their Eyes Were Watching God* (Philadelphia: J. B. Lippincott, 1937); Jessie Fauset, *There Is Confusion* (New York: Boni and Liveright, 1924); and Fauset, *Plum Bun: A Novel without a Moral* (New York: Frederick A. Stokes, 1929).

See Houston A. Baker Jr., *Modernism and the Harlem Renaissance* (Chicago: University of Chicago Press, 1987); George Hutchinson, *The Harlem Renaissance in Black and White* (Cambridge, MA: Harvard University Press, 1995); and Rachael Farebrother, *The Collage Aesthetic in the Harlem Renaissance* (New York: Routledge, 2016).

Langston Hughes, "The Negro Speaks of Rivers," *Crisis*, June 1921, 71.

Langston Hughes, "The Negro Artist and the Racial Mountain," *Nation*, June 23, 1926, 694.

Chapter 5: The making of the modern Civil Rights Movement(s)

Nina Simone, "Mississippi Goddam," *Nina Simone in Concert*, recorded March 21, 1964, Phillips PHM 200–135.

See Nancy Weiss, *Farewell to the Party of Lincoln: Black Politics in the Age of F.D.R.* (Princeton, NJ: Princeton University Press, 1983).

James Goodman, *Stories of Scottsboro* (New York: Pantheon, 1994).

See Raymond Arsenault, *The Sound of Freedom: Marian Anderson, the Lincoln Memorial, and the Concert That Awakened America* (New York: Bloomsbury, 2009).

See Richard Kluger, *Simple Justice: The History of* Brown v. Board of Education *and Black America's Struggle for Equality* (New York: Knopf, 1976).

Jo Ann Gibson Robinson, *The Montgomery Bus Boycott and the Women Who Started It: The Memoir of Jo Ann Gibson Robinson* (Knoxville: University of Tennessee Press, 1987).

Mamie Till-Mobley and Christopher Benson, *Death of Innocence: The Story of the Hate Crime That Changed America* (New York: Random House, 2003); and Elliott J. Gorn, *Let the People See: The Story of Emmett Till* (New York: Oxford University Press, 2018).

Melba Pattillo Beals, *Warriors Don't Cry: The Searing Memoir of the Battle to Integrate Little Rock's Central High* (New York: Simon and Schuster, 1994), 156.

See Barbara Ransby, *Ella Baker and the Black Freedom Movement: A Radical Democratic Vision* (Chapel Hill: University of North Carolina Press, 2003).

Martin Luther King Jr., "Letter from Birmingham Jail," April 16, 1963, in *Why We Can't Wait* (New York: Harper and Row, 1964), 70.

Martin Luther King Jr., "I Have a Dream: Address at March on Washington for Jobs and Freedom," August 28, 1963, in *A Call to Conscience: Landmark Speeches of Martin Luther King Jr.*, ed. Clayborne Carson and Kris Shepard (New York: Grand Central, 2001), 81–82.

Simone, "Mississippi Goddam."

Malcolm X, "Message to the Grassroots," November 10, 1963, Detroit, in *Malcolm X Speaks: Selected Speeches and Statements*, ed. George Breitman (New York: Merit, 1965), 17.

Malcolm X, "The Ballot or the Bullet," April 3, 1964, Cleveland, in *Malcolm X Speaks*, 41.

Malcolm X, "After the Bombing," February 14, 1965, Detroit, in *Malcolm X Speaks*, 164.

See Manning Marable, *Malcolm X: A Life of Reinvention* (New York: Penguin, 2011).

See Taylor Branch, *At Canaan's Edge: America in the King Years, 1965–68* (New York: Simon and Schuster, 2007).

Stokely Carmichael, "SNCC Position Paper on Black Power," *New York Times*, August 5, 1966, quoted in Manning Marable and Leith Mullings, eds., *Let Nobody Turn Us Around: Voices of Resistance, Reform, and Renewal—An African American Anthology* (Lanham, MD: Rowman and Littlefield, 2009), 450.

Chapter 6: The paradoxes of post–civil rights America

See Alondra Nelson, *Body and Soul: The Black Panther Party and the Fight against Medical Discrimination* (Minneapolis: University of Minnesota Press, 2013).

Eldridge Cleaver, *Soul on Ice* (New York: McGraw-Hill, 1967).

Martin Luther King Jr., "Beyond Vietnam," in *A Call to Conscience: Landmark Speeches of Martin Luther King Jr.*, ed. Clayborne Carson and Kris Shepard (New York: Grand Central, 2001), 140, 144.

Taylor Branch, *At Canaan's Edge: America in the King Years, 1965–68* (New York: Simon and Schuster, 2007), 758, 767.

Gil Scott-Heron, "Whitey on the Moon," *Small Talk at 125th and Lenox*, recorded 1970, Flying Dutchman Records FD 10131.

Marvin Gaye, *What's Going On*, recorded June 1, 1970, Tamla T 54201.

See Elaine Brown, *A Taste of Power: A Black Woman's Story* (New York: Pantheon, 1992).

Daniel Patrick Moynihan, "The Negro Family: The Case for National Action," Office of Policy Planning and Research, U.S. Department of Labor, March 1965, 29.

Johnnie Tillmon, "Welfare Is a Women's Issue," *Ms. Magazine*, Spring 1972, 111–16.

See Shirley Chisholm, *Unbought and Unbossed* (Boston: Houghton Mifflin, 1970).

"The Combahee River Collective Statement," in *How We Get Free: Black Feminism and the Combahee River Collective*, ed. Keeanga-Yamahtta Taylor (Chicago: Haymarket Books, 2017), 15, 22–23.

Toni Morrison, *The Bluest Eye* (New York: Holt, Rinehart, and Winston, 1970); Toni Cade Bambara, ed., *The Black Woman:*

An Anthology (New York: New American Library, 1970); and Alice Walker, *Meridian* (New York: Harcourt Brace Jovanovich, 1976).

See Lucius Barker and Ronald Walters, eds., *Jesse Jackson's 1984 Presidential Campaign: Challenge and Change in American Politics* (Urbana: University of Illinois Press, 1989).

Darnell Hunt, *Screening the Los Angeles "Riots": Race, Seeing, and Resistance* (New York: Cambridge University Press, 1997).

Anita Miller, ed., *The Complete Transcripts of the Clarence Thomas–Anita Hill Hearings, October 11, 12, 13, 1991* (Chicago: Academy Chicago, 1994), 23, 154.

Barack Obama, "A More Perfect Union," Philadelphia, March 18, 2008, National Public Radio, transcript, https://www.npr.org/templates/story/story.php?storyId=88478467.

"'New York Post' Political Cartoon Raises Concerns," National Public Radio, February 19, 2009, https://www.npr.org/templates/story/story.php?storyId=100875822.

"Mayor to Quit over Obama Watermelon E-mail," Associated Press, February 27, 2009, http://www.nbcnews.com/id/29423045/ns/us_news-life/t/mayor-quit-over-obama-watermelon-e-mail/#.Xr8q4JNKgdU.

Epilogue: Stony the road we trod

"Transcript of the Baldwin versus Buckley Debate at the Cambridge Union," in Nicholas Buccola, *The Fire Is upon Us: James Baldwin, William F. Buckley Jr., and the Debate over Race in America* (Princeton, NJ: Princeton University Press, 2019), 381.

James Weldon Johnson, "Lift Ev'ry Voice and Sing," 1900, in James Weldon Johnson, *Complete Poems*, ed. Sondra Kathryn Wilson (New York: Penguin, 2000), 110, 109.

See Imani Perry, *May We Forever Stand: A History of the Black National Anthem* (Chapel Hill: University of North Carolina Press, 2018).

Sybrina Fulton and Tracy Martin, *Rest in Power: The Enduring Life of Trayvon Martin* (New York: Spiegel and Grau, 2017).

Jelani Cobb, "The Matter of Black Lives," *New Yorker*, March 14, 2016, https://www.newyorker.com/magazine/2016/03/14/where-is-black-lives-matter-headed.

See Chad Williams, Kidada E. Williams, and Keisha Blain, eds., *Charleston Syllabus: Readings on Race, Racism, and Racial Violence* (Athens: University of Georgia Press, 2016).

Glenn Thrush and Maggie Haberman, "Trump Gives White Supremacists an Equivocal Boost," *New York Times*, August 15, 2017, https://www.nytimes.com/2017/08/15/us/politics/trump-charlottesville-white-nationalists.html.

Lonnie G. Bunch III, *A Fool's Errand: Creating the National Museum of African American History and Culture in the Age of Bush, Obama, and Trump* (Washington, DC: Smithsonian Books, 2019).

Campbell Robertson, "A Lynching Memorial Is Opening: The Country Has Never Seen Anything Like It," *New York Times*, April 25, 2018, https://www.nytimes.com/2018/04/25/us/lynching-memorial-alabama.html.

Further reading

Alexander, Michelle. *The New Jim Crow: Mass Incarceration in the Age of Colorblindness*. New York: New Press, 2012.

Allen, James, Hilton Als, John Lewis, and Leon F. Litwack. *Without Sanctuary: Lynching Photography in America*. Santa Fe, NM: Twin Palms, 2000.

Arsenault, Raymond. *The Sound of Freedom: Marian Anderson, the Lincoln Memorial, and the Concert That Awakened America*. New York: Bloomsbury, 2009.

Baker, Houston A. Jr. *Modernism and the Harlem Renaissance*. Chicago: University of Chicago Press, 1987.

Baldwin, James. *The Fire Next Time*. New York: Dial Press, 1963.

Baptist, Edward. *The Half Has Never Been Told: Slavery and the Making of American Capitalism*. New York: Basic Books, 2014.

Barker, Lucius, and Ronald Walters, eds. *Jesse Jackson's 1984 Presidential Campaign: Challenge and Change in American Politics*. Urbana: University of Illinois Press, 1989.

Bates, Beth. *Pullman Porters and the Rise of Black Protest Politics*. Chapel Hill: University of North Carolina Press, 2001.

Bay, Mia. *To Tell the Truth Freely: The Life of Ida B. Wells*. New York: Hill and Wang, 2009.

Beals, Melba Pattillo. *Warriors Don't Cry: The Searing Memoir of the Battle to Integrate Little Rock's Central High*. New York: Simon and Schuster, 1994.

Bederman, Gail. *Manliness and Civilization: A Cultural History of Gender and Race in the United States, 1880–1917*. Chicago: University of Chicago Press, 2005.

Berlin, Ira. *Generations of Captivity: A History of African-American Slaves*. Cambridge, MA: Harvard University Press, 2003.

Berlin, Ira. *Many Thousands Gone: The First Two Centuries of Slavery in North America*. Cambridge, MA: Harvard University Press, 1998.

Bernstein, Iver. *The New York City Draft Riots: Their Significance for American Society and Politics in the Age of the Civil War*. New York: Oxford University Press, 1991.

Berry, Daina Ramey. *The Price for Their Pound of Flesh: The Value of the Enslaved, from Womb to Grave, in the Building of a Nation*. Boston: Beacon Press, 2017.

Blatt, Martin H., Thomas J. Brown, and Donald Yacovone, eds. *Hope and Glory: Essays on the Legacy of the 54th Massachusetts Regiment*. Amherst: University of Massachusetts Press, 2001.

Blight, David. *Frederick Douglass: Prophet of Freedom*. New York: W. W. Norton, 2018.

Blight, David. *Race and Reunion: The Civil War in American Memory*. Cambridge, MA: Harvard University Press, 2001.

Branch, Taylor. *At Canaan's Edge: America in the King Years, 1965–68*. New York: Simon and Schuster, 2007.

Brooks, Gwendolyn. *The Essential Gwendolyn Brooks*. Edited by Elizabeth Alexander. New York: Library of America, 2005.

Brown, Elaine. *A Taste of Power: A Black Woman's Story*. New York: Pantheon Books, 1992.

Brown, Elsa Barkley. "Womanist Consciousness: Maggie Lena Walker and the Independent Order of Saint Luke." *Signs* 14 (1989): 610–33.

Brown, John. *Testimonies of Capt. John Brown, at Harper's Ferry, with his Address to the Court*. New York: American Anti-Slavery Society, 1860.

Brown, Sterling. *Southern Road*. New York: Harcourt, Brace, and Company, 1932.

Buccola, Nicholas. *The Fire Is upon Us: James Baldwin, William F. Buckley Jr., and the Debate over Race in America*. Princeton, NJ: Princeton University Press, 2019.

Bunch, Lonnie G., III. *A Fool's Errand: Creating the National Museum of African American History and Culture in the Age of Bush, Obama, and Trump*. Washington, DC: Smithsonian Books, 2019.

Cabeza de Vaca, Álvar Núñez. *The Narrative of Cabeza de Vaca*. Translated and edited by Rolena Adorno and Patrick Charles Pautz. Lincoln: University of Nebraska Press, 2003.

Cade Bambara, Toni, ed. *The Black Woman: An Anthology*. New York: New American Library, 1970.

Camp, Stephanie. *Closer to Freedom: Enslaved Women and Everyday Resistance in the Plantation South*. Chapel Hill: University of North Carolina Press, 2004.

Carretta, Vincent. *Phillis Wheatley: Biography of a Genius in Bondage*. Athens: University of Georgia Press, 2011.

Carson, Clayborne, and Kris Shepard, eds. *A Call to Conscience: Landmark Speeches of Martin Luther King Jr*. New York: Grand Central, 2001.

Chisholm, Shirley. *Unbought and Unbossed*. Boston: Houghton Mifflin, 1970.

Cimbala, Paul, and Randall Miller, eds. *The Freedmen's Bureau and Reconstruction: Reconsiderations*. New York: Fordham University Press, 1999.

Clarke, John Henrik, ed., with Amy Jacques Garvey. *Marcus Garvey and the Vision of Africa*. New York: Vintage, 1974.

Cleaver, Eldridge. *Soul on Ice*. 1967. Reprint, New York: Delta Trader Paperbacks, 1999.

Cleaver, Kathleen, and George Kastlaficas, eds. *Liberation, Imagination, and the Black Panther Party: A New Look at the Panthers and Their Legacy*. New York: Routledge, 2001.

Cobb, Jelani. "The Matter of Black Lives." *New Yorker*, March 14, 2016. https://www.newyorker.com/magazine/2016/03/14/where-is-black-lives-matter-headed.

Cobleigh, Rolfe. "Fighting a Vicious Film: Protest against 'The Birth of a Nation.'" Boston Branch of the NAACP, 1915.

Collins, Patricia Hill. *Black Feminist Thought: Knowledge, Consciousness, and the Politics of Empowerment*. New York: Routledge, 2008.

Cooper, Anna Julia. *A Voice from the South*. Xenia, OH: Aldine Printing House, 1892.

Davis, Angela. *Women, Race, and Class*. New York: Random House, 1981.

Davis, David Brion. *Inhuman Bondage: The Rise and Fall of Slavery in the New World*. New York: Oxford University Press, 2006.

Delany, Martin. *The Condition, Elevation, Emigration, and Destiny of the Colored People of the United States, Politically Considered*. Philadelphia: Published by the author, 1852.

Downs, Jim. *Sick from Freedom: African-American Illness and Suffering during the Civil War and Reconstruction*. New York: Oxford University Press, 2012.

Du Bois, W. E. B. *Black Reconstruction in America: An Essay toward a History of the Part Which Black Folk Played in the Attempt to Reconstruct Democracy in America, 1860–1880*. New York: Harcourt, Brace, and Company, 1935.

Du Bois, W. E. B. "Close Ranks." *Crisis*, July 1918, 111–14.

Du Bois, W. E. B. *Dusk of Dawn: An Essay toward an Autobiography of a Race Concept*. New York: Schocken Books, 1940.

Du Bois, W. E. B. *The Philadelphia Negro*. Philadelphia: University of Pennsylvania Press, 1898.

Du Bois, W. E. B. "Returning Soldiers." *Crisis*, May 1919, 13–14.

Du Bois, W. E. B. *The Souls of Black Folk*. Chicago: A. C. McClurg, 1903.

Eltis, David. *The Rise of African Slavery in the Americas*. New York: Cambridge University Press, 2000.

Eltis, David. Voyages: The Trans-Atlantic Slave Trade Database. https://slavevoyages.org.

Equiano, Olaudah. *The Interesting Narrative of the Life of Olaudah Equiano, or Gustavus Vassa, the African. Written by Himself*. London: Printed by the author, 1789.

Falconbridge, Alexander. *An Account of the Slave Trade on the Coast of Africa*. London: J. Phillips, 1788.

Farebrother, Rachael. *The Collage Aesthetic in the Harlem Renaissance*. New York: Routledge, 2016.

Fauset, Jessie. *Plum Bun: A Novel without a Moral*. New York: Frederick A. Stokes, 1929.

Fauset, Jessie. *There Is Confusion*. New York: Boni and Liveright, 1924.

Faust, Drew Gilpin. *This Republic of Suffering: Death and the American Civil War*. New York: Knopf, 2008.

Feimster, Crystal. *Southern Horrors: Women and the Politics of Rape and Lynching*. Cambridge, MA: Harvard University Press, 2009.

Feldstein, Ruth. *How It Feels to Be Free: Black Women Entertainers and the Civil Rights Movement*. New York: Oxford University Press, 2013.

Foner, Eric. *The Fiery Trial: Abraham Lincoln and American Slavery*. New York: W. W. Norton, 2010.

Foner, Eric. *Reconstruction: America's Unfinished Revolution, 1863–1877*. New York: Harper and Row, 1988.

Foner, Philip, ed. *The Life and Writings of Frederick Douglass*. Vol. 2, *Pre–Civil War Decade, 1850–1860*. New York: International, 1950.

Ford, Richard Thompson. *The Race Card*. New York: Farrar, Straus and Giroux, 2008.

Franklin, John Hope, and Evelyn Brooks Higginbotham. *From Slavery to Freedom: A History of African Americans*. 9th ed. New York: McGraw-Hill, 2011.

Franklin, John Hope, and Loren Schweninger. *Runaway Slaves: Rebels on the Plantation*. New York: Oxford University Press, 1999.

Fulton, Sybrina, and Tracy Martin. *Rest in Power: The Enduring Life of Trayvon Martin*. New York: Spiegel and Grau, 2017.

Gaines, Kevin. *Uplifting the Race: Black Leadership, Politics, and Culture in the Twentieth Century*. Chapel Hill: University of North Carolina Press, 1996.

Gaye, Marvin. *What's Going On*. Recorded June 1, 1970. Tamla T 54201.

Genovese, Eugene D. *From Rebellion to Revolution: Afro-American Slave Revolts in the Making of the Modern World*. Baton Rouge: Louisiana State University Press, 1979.

Gilmore, Glenda. *Gender and Jim Crow: Women and the Politics of White Supremacy in North Carolina, 1893–1920*. Chapel Hill: University of North Carolina Press, 1996.

Glymph, Thavolia. *Out of the House of Bondage: The Transformation of the Plantation Household*. New York: Cambridge University Press, 2008.

Goodman, James. *Stories of Scottsboro*. New York: Pantheon Books, 1994.

Gordon-Reed, Annette. *The Hemingses of Monticello: An American Family*. New York: Norton, 2009.

Gorn, Elliott J. *Let the People See: The Story of Emmett Till*. New York: Oxford University Press, 2018.

Grant, Colin. *Negro with a Hat: The Rise and Fall of Marcus Garvey*. New York: Oxford University Press, 2010.

Grossman, James. *Land of Hope: Chicago, Black Southerners, and the Great Migration*. Chicago: University of Chicago Press, 1989.

Hahn, Steven. *A Nation under Our Feet: Black Political Struggles in the Rural South from Slavery to the Great Migration*. Cambridge, MA: Harvard University Press, 2003.

Hall, Jacquelyn Dowd. "The Long Civil Rights Movement and the Political Uses of the Past." *Journal of American History* 91, no. 4 (2005): 1233–63.

Harlan, Louis R., ed. *The Booker T. Washington Papers*. Vol. 3, *1889–95*. Urbana: University of Illinois Press, 1974.

Harris, Leslie. *In the Shadow of Slavery: African Americans in New York, 1626–1863.* Chicago: University of Chicago Press, 2003.

Hartman, Saidiya. *Scenes of Subjection: Terror, Slavery, and Self-Making in Nineteenth-Century America.* New York: Oxford University Press, 1997.

Higginbotham, Evelyn Brooks. *Righteous Discontent: The Women's Movement in the Black Baptist Church, 1880–1920.* Cambridge, MA: Harvard University Press, 1993.

Hill, Anita. "The Smear This Time." *New York Times,* October 2, 2007.

Holiday, Billie, vocalist. "Strange Fruit." Lyrics by Abel Meeropol. Recorded April 20, 1939, Commodore Records C-526.

Holloway, Jonathan. *Confronting the Veil: Abram Harris Jr., E. Franklin Frazier, and Ralph Bunche, 1919–1941.* Chapel Hill: University of North Carolina Press, 2002.

Holt, Thomas. *Children of Fire: A History of African Americans.* New York: Hill and Wang, 2010.

Horton, James Oliver, and Lois E. Horton, eds. *Slavery and Public History: The Tough Stuff of American Memory.* Chapel Hill: University of North Carolina Press, 2008.

Huggins, Nathan. *Black Odyssey: The African-American Ordeal in Slavery.* New York: Vintage, 1990.

Hughes, Langston. "The Negro Artist and the Racial Mountain." *Nation,* June 23, 1926, 692–94.

Hughes, Langston. "The Negro Speaks of Rivers." *Crisis,* June 1921, 71.

Hunt, Darnell. *Screening the Los Angeles "Riots": Race, Seeing, and Resistance.* New York: Cambridge University Press, 1997.

Hunter, Tera. *To 'Joy My Freedom: Southern Black Women's Lives and Labors after the Civil War.* Cambridge, MA: Harvard University Press, 1997.

Hurston, Zora Neale. *Mules and Men.* Philadelphia: J. B. Lippincott, 1935.

Hurston, Zora Neale. *Their Eyes Were Watching God.* Philadelphia: J. B. Lippincott, 1937.

Hutchinson, George. *The Harlem Renaissance in Black and White.* Cambridge, MA: Harvard University Press, 1995.

Jacobs, Harriet. *Incidents in the Life of a Slave Girl.* Boston: Published for the author, 1861.

Janiskee, Bob. "Sullivan's Island Was the African-American Ellis Island." *National Parks Traveler,* March 4, 2009. https://www.nationalparkstraveler.org/2009/03/sullivan-s-island-african-american-ellis-island.

Jefferson, Thomas. *Notes on the State of Virginia.* 1785. Philadelphia: Prichard and Hall, 1787.

Jennings, Thelma. "'Us Colored Women Had to Go through a Plenty': Sexual Exploitation of African-American Slave Women." *Journal of Women's History* 1, no. 3 (1999): 45–74.

Johnson, James Weldon. *Complete Poems.* Edited by Sondra Kathryn Wilson. New York: Penguin, 2000.

Johnson, Walter. *Soul by Soul: Life Inside the Antebellum Slave Market.* Cambridge, MA: Harvard University Press, 2001.

Keiler, Allan. *Marian Anderson: A Singer's Journey.* Urbana: University of Illinois Press, 2006.

Kelley, Robin D. G. "'We Are Not What We Seem': Rethinking Black Working-Class Opposition in the Jim Crow South." *Journal of American History* 80, no. 1 (1993): 75–112.

Kelley, Robin D. G., and Earl Lewis. *To Make Our World Anew.* New York: Oxford University Press, 2005.

King, Martin Luther Jr. *Why We Can't Wait.* New York: Harper and Row, 1964.

Kluger, Richard. *Simple Justice: The History of* Brown v. Board of Education *and Black America's Struggle for Equality.* New York: Knopf, 1976.

Lee, Chana Kai. *For Freedom's Sake: The Life of Fannie Lou Hamer.* Urbana: University of Illinois Press, 2000.

Lemire, Elise. *Black Walden: Slavery and Its Aftermath in Concord, Massachusetts.* Philadelphia: University of Pennsylvania Press, 2008.

Litwack, Leon. *Been in the Storm So Long: The Aftermath of Slavery.* New York: Knopf, 1979.

Locke, Alain, ed. *The New Negro: An Interpretation.* New York: A. and C. Boni, 1925.

Logan, Rayford. *The Negro in American Life and Thought: The Nadir, 1877–1901.* New York: Dial Press, 1952.

Lorini, Alessandra. *Rituals of Race: American Public Culture and the Search for Racial Democracy.* Charlottesville: University of Virginia Press, 1999.

Maddock Dillon, Elizabeth, and Michael Drexler, eds. *The Haitian Revolution and the Early United States: Histories, Textualities, Geographies.* Philadelphia: University of Pennsylvania Press, 2016.

Marable, Manning. *Malcolm X: A Life of Reinvention.* New York: Penguin, 2011.

Marable, Manning, and Leith Mullings, eds. *Let Nobody Turn Us Around: Voices of Resistance, Reform, and Renewal—An African*

American Anthology. Lanham, MD: Rowman and
Littlefield, 2009.

Martin, Waldo, and Joshua Bloom. *Black against Empire: The History
and Politics of the Black Panther Party.* Berkeley: University of
California Press, 2016.

McGuire, Danielle. *At the Dark End of the Street: Black Women,
Rape, and Resistance—A New History of the Civil Rights
Movement from Rosa Parks to the Rise of Black Power.* New York:
Penguin, 2011.

McPherson, James. *Battle Cry of Freedom: The Civil War Era.* New
York: Oxford University Press, 1988.

McPherson, James. *Ordeal by Fire: The Civil War and Reconstruction.*
New York: Knopf, 1982.

Miller, Anita, ed. *The Complete Transcripts of the Clarence Thomas–
Anita Hill Hearings, October 11, 12, 13, 1991.* Chicago: Academy
Chicago, 1994.

Morgan, Edmund. *American Slavery, American Freedom: The Ordeal
of Colonial Virginia.* New York: W. W. Norton, 1975.

Morrison, Toni. *Beloved.* New York: Knopf, 1987.

Morrison, Toni. *The Bluest Eye.* New York: Holt, Rinehart, and
Winston, 1970.

Moynihan, Daniel Patrick. "The Negro Family: The Case for National
Action." Office of Policy Planning and Research, US Department of
Labor, March 1965.

Mullane, Deirdre. *Crossing the Danger Water: Three Hundred Years of
African-American Writing.* New York: Anchor, 1993.

Nadasen, Premilla. "Expanding the Boundaries of the Women's
Movement: Black Feminism and the Struggle for Welfare Rights."
Feminist Studies 28, no. 2 (2002): 271–303.

Nelson, Alondra. *Body and Soul: The Black Panther Party and the
Fight against Medical Discrimination.* Minneapolis: University of
Minnesota Press, 2013.

Northrup, Solomon. *Twelve Years a Slave: Narrative of Solomon
Northup, a Citizen of New-York, Kidnapped in Washington City in
1841, and Rescued in 1853, from a Cotton Plantation near the Red
River, in Louisiana.* Auburn, NY: Derby and Miller, 1853.

Obama, Barack. "A More Perfect Union." Philadelphia, March 18,
2008. National Public Radio, transcript. https://www.npr.org/
templates/story/story.php?storyId=88,478,467.

O'Malley, Michael. *Face Value: The Entwined Histories of Money and
Race in America.* Chicago: University of Chicago Press, 2012.

Painter, Nell Irvin. *Sojourner Truth: A Life, A Symbol.* New York:
W. W. Norton, 1996.

Payne, Charles. *I've Got the Light of Freedom: The Organizing
Tradition and the Mississippi Freedom Struggle.* Berkeley:
University of California Press, 1995.

Perry, Imani. *May We Forever Stand: A History of the Black
National Anthem.* Chapel Hill: University of North Carolina
Press, 2018.

Ransby, Barbara. *Ella Baker and the Black Freedom Movement:
A Radical Democratic Vision.* Chapel Hill: University of North
Carolina Press, 2003.

Ransby, Barbara. "Fear of a Black Feminist Planet." In *Civil Rights
Since 1787: A Reader on the Black Struggle.* Edited by Jonathan
Birnbaum and Clarence Taylor. New York: New York University
Press, 2000.

Rediker, Marcus. *The Slave Ship: A Human History.* New York:
Penguin Books, 2014.

Robertson, David. *Denmark Vesey: The Buried Story of America's
Largest Slave Rebellion and the Man Who Led It.* New York:
Knopf, 1999.

Robinson, Jo Ann Gibson. *The Montgomery Bus Boycott and the
Women Who Started It: The Memoir of Jo Ann Gibson Robinson.*
Knoxville: University of Tennessee Press, 1987.

Scott, William R. *Upon These Shores: Themes in the African-American
Experience, 1600 to the Present.* New York: Routledge, 1999.

Scott-Heron, Gil. "Whitey on the Moon." *Small Talk at 125th and
Lenox.* Recorded 1970. Flying Dutchman Records FD 10131.

Shange, Ntozake. *For Colored Girls Who Have Considered Suicide
When the Rainbow Was Enuf.* New York: Macmillan, 1977.

Simone, Nina. "Mississippi Goddam." *Nina Simone in Concert.*
Recorded March 21, 1964. Phillips PHM 200–135.

Sinha, Manisha. *The Slave's Cause: A History of Abolition.* New
Haven, CT: Yale University Press, 2016.

Smallwood, Stephanie. *Saltwater Slavery: A Middle Passage from
Africa to American Diaspora.* Cambridge, MA: Harvard University
Press, 2007.

Stewart, Maria W. *Maria W. Stewart, America's First Black Woman
Political Writer: Essays and Speeches.* Edited by Marilyn
Richardson. Bloomington: Indiana University Press, 1987.

Stowe, Harriet Beecher. *Uncle Tom's Cabin.* Boston:
John P. Jewett, 1852.

Sugrue, Thomas. *Sweet Land of Liberty: The Forgotten Struggle for Civil Rights in the North*. New York: Random House, 2008.

Sullivan, Patricia. *Days of Hope: Race and Democracy in the New Deal Era*. Chapel Hill: University of North Carolina Press, 1996.

Taylor, Eric. *If We Must Die: Shipboard Insurrections in the Era of the Atlantic Slave Trade*. Baton Rouge: Louisiana State University Press, 2009.

Taylor, Keeanga-Yamahtta, ed. *How We Get Free: Black Feminism and the Combahee River Collective*. Chicago: Haymarket Books, 2017.

Theoharis, Jeanne. *A More Beautiful and Terrible History: The Uses and Misuses of Civil Rights History*. Boston: Beacon Press, 2019.

Theoharis, Jeanne. *The Rebellious Life of Mrs. Rosa Parks*. Boston: Beacon Press, 2014.

Tillet, Salamishah. *Sites of Slavery: Citizenship and Racial Democracy in the Post–Civil Rights Imagination*. Durham, NC: Duke University Press, 2012.

Till-Mobley, Mamie, and Christopher Benson. *Death of Innocence: The Story of the Hate Crime That Changed America*. New York: Random House, 2003.

Tillmon, Johnnie. "Welfare Is a Women's Issue." *Ms. Magazine*, Spring 1972, 111–16.

Trethewey, Natasha. *Native Guard: Poems*. Boston: Houghton Mifflin, 2006.

Tuttle, William. *Race Riot*. Champaign: University of Illinois Press, 1970.

Tyson, Timothy. *Radio Free Dixie: Robert F. Williams and the Roots of Black Power*. Chapel Hill: University of North Carolina Press, 2001.

Vogel, Shane. *The Scene of Harlem Cabaret*. Chicago: University of Chicago Press, 2009.

Walker, Alice. *Meridian*. New York: Harcourt Brace Jovanovich, 1976.

Walker, David. *Walker's Appeal in Four Articles; Together with a Preamble, to the Coloured Citizens of the World, but in Particular, and Very Expressly, to Those of the United States of America*. Boston: David Walker, 1829.

Washington, Booker T. *Up from Slavery*. New York: Doubleday, 1901.

Weiss, Nancy. *Farewell to the Party of Lincoln: Black Politics in the Age of F.D.R.* Princeton, NJ: Princeton University Press, 1983.

Wheatley, Phillis. *Poems on Various Subjects, Religious and Moral*. London: Archibald Bell, 1773.

White, Deborah Gray, Mia Bay, and Waldo Martin Jr. *Freedom on My Mind: A History of African Americans with Documents*. Boston: Bedford/St. Martin's, 2012.

Wilkerson, Isabel. *The Warmth of Other Suns: The Epic Story of America's Great Migration*. New York: Random House, 2010.

Williams, Chad, Kidada E. Williams, and Keisha Blain, eds. *Charleston Syllabus: Readings on Race, Racism, and Racial Violence*. Athens: University of Georgia Press, 2016.

Williams, Heather. *American Slavery: A Very Short Introduction*. New York: Oxford University Press, 2014.

X, Malcolm. *Malcolm X Speaks: Selected Speeches and Statements*. Edited by George Breitman. New York: Merit, 1965.

Index

For the benefit of digital users, indexed terms that span two pages (e.g., 52–53) may, on occasion, appear on only one of those pages.

Figures are indicated by *f* following the page number.

Index